This journal belongs to

Published by Barbour Books, an imprint of Barbour Publishing, Inc., 1810 Barbour Drive, Uhrichsville, Ohio 44683, www.barbourbooks.com

Our mission is to inspire the world with the life-changing message of the Bible.

 Member of the
Evangelical Christian
Publishers Association

Printed in China.

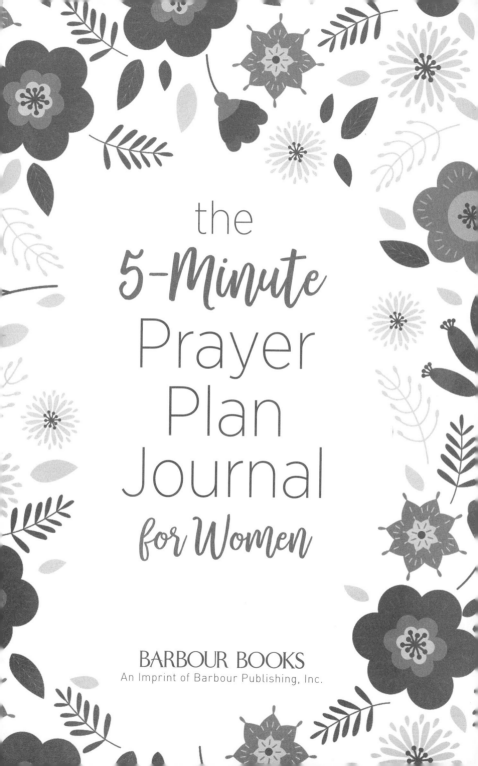

the
5-Minute
Prayer
Plan
Journal
for Women

BARBOUR BOOKS
An Imprint of Barbour Publishing, Inc.

denial. Maybe there have been times when fear paralyzed you and kept you silent. How did you feel afterward? What did you do to restore your strength as a witness?

....

....

....

Peter was forgiven by Christ for his denial. He didn't allow his past failures to keep him from finding his life in Christ. How can you forget the past and move forward in your faith?

....

....

....

Ask God to direct you to those who need to hear His message.

....

....

....

Jesus, sometimes I'm afraid of what others may think of me and my faith. It's not popular to take a stand as a Christian right now. I fool myself into thinking I'm just being wise in not saying anything. Fear keeps me silent when I need to take a stand for You. Later, shame overwhelms me, and I feel so unworthy of Your love. At those times, I feel like a failure. I need Your help to become a stronger witness for You. Help me to surrender my fear to You so I can become what You would have me to be. I want to stand before the Father knowing You will confess me before Him as one of Yours.

Come unto Me

At that time Jesus answered and said, I thank thee, O Father, Lord of heaven and earth, because thou hast hid these things from the wise and prudent, and hast revealed them unto babes. . . . All things are delivered unto me of my Father: and no man knoweth the Son, but the Father; neither knoweth any man the Father, save the Son, and he to whomsoever the Son will reveal him. Come unto me, all ye that labour and are heavy laden, and I will give you rest. Take my yoke upon you, and learn of me; for I am meek and lowly in heart: and ye shall find rest unto your souls. For my yoke is easy, and my burden is light.

MATTHEW 11:25, 27–30 KJV

We cannot know the Father without the Son revealing Him to us. The Son reveals the Father to us as we come to Him, drawing closer to Him in a more intimate relationship. What are some ways you can draw closer to Christ?

Jesus said all things had been delivered or given to Him by His Father. What does this mean to you as a Christian?

If we go to Christ, He gives us rest from our burdens. What kind of burdens are you bearing?

....

....

....

....

The yoke of the world is heavy, but Jesus said His yoke is easy and His burden is light. What kind of yoke are you wearing today?

....

....

....

....

Are you experiencing stress or frustration? Do you need rest for your soul? How can you find this rest?

....

....

....

....

Jesus, I want to know You and the Father in all Your fullness. I need more of You. I'm weary of my life. Too many burdens rest on my shoulders. I can't do this anymore. Your Word tells me I can come to You, learn more about You, and find rest from all this. Help me to find this rest You have so freely offered. Show me how to surrender my burdens to You. I've tried in the past, but I always go back to worrying about them instead of letting You take care of them. Help me to trust You with my problems. Take the yoke I've been wearing and replace it with Your yoke.

Walking Worthy of the Lord

For this cause we also, since the day we heard it, do not cease to pray for you, and to desire that ye might be filled with the knowledge of his will in all wisdom and spiritual understanding; that ye might walk worthy of the Lord unto all pleasing, being fruitful in every good work, and increasing in the knowledge of God; strengthened with all might, according to his glorious power, unto all patience and longsuffering with joyfulness; giving thanks unto the Father, which hath made us meet to be partakers of the inheritance of the saints in light: who hath delivered us from the power of darkness, and hath translated us into the kingdom of his dear Son.

Colossians 1:9–13 KJV

What does it mean to be filled with the knowledge of God's will in wisdom and spiritual understanding?

....

....

....

....

As Christians, our focus should be on pleasing God. How do we "walk worthy of the Lord unto all pleasing"? What are some areas you need to improve on?

....

....

....

....

Good works naturally flow from the Christian who seeks to please the Lord and become fruitful in the kingdom, but sometimes we allow life's responsibilities to interfere with our fruit bearing. What are some ways you can balance your daily routine and still be fruitful in your Christian walk?

....

....

....

How are you striving to increase in the knowledge of God?

....

....

....

We can be strengthened by God according to His glorious power. How are you allowing God to strengthen you day by day?

....

....

....

Jesus, fill me with the knowledge of Your will. My will gets in the way too often even when I know it shouldn't. Help me to bring my will under subjection to Your will, realizing You always know best. When I choose my will over Yours, I always get in trouble. I can't do this by myself. I need wisdom and spiritual understanding that can only be supplied by You. Help me in the choices I make every day. I need to make decisions that are pleasing to You. Open my understanding to know Your will. Help me to live my life in a manner that is worthy of You as I strive to be a fruitful Christian. Strengthen me by Your glorious power so that I might be all I can be for You.

Feeling Content

But I rejoiced in the Lord greatly, that now at the last your care of me hath flourished again; wherein ye were also careful, but ye lacked opportunity. Not that I speak in respect of want: for I have learned, in whatsoever state I am, therewith to be content. I know both how to be abased, and I know how to abound: every where and in all things I am instructed both to be full and to be hungry, both to abound and to suffer need. I can do all things through Christ which strengtheneth me. . . . But my God shall supply all your need according to his riches in glory by Christ Jesus.

PHILIPPIANS 4:10–13, 19 KJV

What state are you in today?

....

....

....

....

If you're not content with your life, is there something you know is keeping you unhappy? Is there something you can do to improve the situation?

....

....

....

....

If you're not content, are you allowing what others have to influence your thoughts? Is your discontentment the result of a real need, or is it based on something you want that may or may not be a necessity?

....

....

....

Verse 19 says that God will supply all our needs according to His riches in glory by Christ Jesus. How does this apply to your being content with life?

....

....

....

Paul wrote that he had learned to accept being full or being hungry. How can this apply to your spiritual life as well as the physical?

....

....

....

Jesus, I know I shouldn't feel discontented, but there are things I would like to have. It's hard to see others who have so much when all I need is just a little of what they have. Forgive me, I know that's wrong. I wish I could be more like Paul. He said he had learned to be content in whatever state he was in, but I'm just not there yet. Help me to recognize the blessings I do have and to be thankful for them. Help me to remember that everything here is temporary, not eternal. Give me the strength I need to face whatever comes my way. Your Word says You will supply all my need. Help me to accept Your promise and have faith that You will take care of whatever situation I find myself in.

Let the Peace of God Rule

Therefore, as God's chosen people, holy and dearly loved, clothe yourselves with compassion, kindness, humility, gentleness and patience. Bear with each other and forgive one another if any of you has a grievance against someone. Forgive as the Lord forgave you. And over all these virtues put on love, which binds them all together in perfect unity. Let the peace of Christ rule in your hearts, since as members of one body you were called to peace. And be thankful. Let the message of Christ dwell among you richly as you teach and admonish one another with all wisdom through psalms, hymns, and songs from the Spirit, singing to God with gratitude in your hearts.

Colossians 3:12–16 niv

As God's people, we're to clothe ourselves with such qualities as compassion, kindness, humility, gentleness, and patience. Do you feel you might be lacking in any of these? If so, which ones do you need to work on? Ask God to help you be more like Him.

....

....

....

....

We're instructed to bear with and forgive one another. What are some ways we should bear with each other in daily life?

....

....

....

....

Sometimes we feel we're doing all the bearing and forgiving and the other person isn't doing his or her part. How should we deal with these feelings?

....

....

....

As members of the body of Christ, we're called to peace. How can we pursue peace when others seem determined to create strife? Pray for those who create strife.

....

....

....

What is the message of Christ, and how are you sharing it with others? Ask God to lead you to those who need to hear the Gospel.

....

....

....

Lord, I need to be more like You. Show me how to do this. It's hard to bear with some people, and You know those I have a hard time with. Sometimes I feel angry toward them. Help me to love them through You. If there's something in my heart against anyone, forgive me. You've forgiven me of so much; let me show that same forgiveness to others. Fill me with Your love, and let Your peace rule in my life. Help me to pursue that peace with others even when they don't agree with me. Let the message of Christ dwell within me, and show me how to share that message with others.

Rooted and Grounded in Christ

For this cause I bow my knees unto the Father of our Lord Jesus Christ, of whom the whole family in heaven and earth is named, that he would grant you, according to the riches of his glory, to be strengthened with might by his Spirit in the inner man; that Christ may dwell in your hearts by faith; that ye, being rooted and grounded in love, may be able to comprehend with all saints what is the breadth, and length, and depth, and height; and to know the love of Christ, which passeth knowledge, that ye might be filled with all the fulness of God. Now unto him that is able to do exceeding abundantly above all that we ask or think, according to the power that worketh in us.
EPHESIANS 3:14–20 KJV

What does it mean to you to be "strengthened in the inner man" by God's Spirit?

....

....

....

Christ dwells within our hearts by faith. How can we know that He has taken up residence in our lives?

....

....

In what way can you become more rooted and grounded in God's love?

....

....

In our natural minds, it's hard to grasp the love of Christ. It's greater than any earthly knowledge we might obtain. How does God help us to comprehend His love for us?

....

....

....

God is able to do exceeding abundantly above what we even think or know to ask, but it's according to the power that works in us. That power comes from Him. Ask Him to increase His power in your life.

....

....

....

Paul prayed the prayer in Ephesians 3:14–19 for the Ephesian church. Why not pray this same prayer for yourself and those around you?

....

....

....

Lord, sometimes I feel weak spiritually. I know I need to be strengthened by Your Spirit. I need more of Your power working in my life. Help me become more rooted and grounded in You and Your Word so that I may know You better. There are so many things I don't understand, but I know You are able to help me understand them. I want to be filled with all You have for me. Your Word tells me that You can do exceeding abundantly more than I can ask or think, so I know that nothing is impossible for You.

Be of Good Cheer

*And straightway Jesus constrained his disciples to get into
a ship, and to go before him unto the other side, while he sent
the multitudes away. And when he had sent the multitudes away,
he went up into a mountain apart to pray: and when the evening
was come, he was there alone. But the ship was now in the midst
of the sea, tossed with waves: for the wind was contrary. And in
the fourth watch of the night Jesus went unto them, walking on
the sea. And when the disciples saw him walking on the sea,
they were troubled, saying, It is a spirit; and they cried out
for fear. But straightway Jesus spake unto them, saying,
Be of good cheer; it is I; be not afraid.*

MATTHEW 14:22–27 KJV

Jesus sent the disciples to the other side of the sea where they encountered a terrible storm. He knew the storm was coming, so why do you think He sent them into it?

....

....

....

....

The disciples were afraid: they cried out in fear. We all face times when we're afraid. What should we do when fear overwhelms us, paralyzing our minds?

....

....

....

....

Sometimes fear is a good thing, especially when our lives are in danger. How should we deal with this kind of fear?

....

....

....

Jesus can calm any storm we might face. Are you facing something in your life right now that only He can take care of? What are some ways you can release it to Him?

....

....

....

Storms are inevitable in this life. How can we prepare for those times when they come?

....

....

....

Jesus, sometimes I'm frightened of the storms that come my way, both spiritual and physical. Fear paralyzes me and keeps me from being able to think clearly. Give me victory over this fear. Help me to know that You're always with me, no matter what I'm facing. I don't always understand why these problems happen, but give me the faith to trust You no matter what. Help me to rely on You and not on my own devices. Help me to listen for Your voice when the winds of trouble are blowing. Help me to know that You are near. Show me Your power and Your strength so that I might be what You would have me to be.

My Help Comes from the Lord

I lift up my eyes to the mountains—where does my help come from? My help comes from the LORD, the Maker of heaven and earth. He will not let your foot slip—he who watches over you will not slumber; indeed, he who watches over Israel will neither slumber nor sleep. The LORD watches over you—the LORD is your shade at your right hand; the sun will not harm you by day, nor the moon by night. The LORD will keep you from all harm— he will watch over your life; the LORD will watch over your coming and going both now and forevermore.

PSALM 121:1-8 NIV

Sometimes we look to natural sources for help first. Is it wrong to rely on human help, or are there times when that's the way we receive what we need? How can we focus more on the Lord and the help He wants to give us?

....

....

....

....

God is the Master Creator. He has no trouble watching over the universe. Does doubt ever creep in and destroy your confidence in His ability to control your world?

....

....

....

....

The scripture tells us that God "will not let your foot slip." Does this mean we will never have a problem or an accident? What does this verse mean to you?

....

....

....

How do we answer those who question why bad things happen in the world? Do you ever face those same questions in your mind? Where do you go for answers?

....

....

....

We must place our trust in God, knowing that whatever comes our way, He will be there for us. If you stumble sometimes or face misfortune, what are some things you can do to begin again?

....

....

....

Lord, I know You're my source of help, but sometimes You're not the first one I call on. Sometimes I depend on my own ability to fix the problem only to realize that my abilities are inadequate. Show me how to depend on You in all things. Thank You for watching over me even when I'm going about my day with my mind on other things. Thank You for taking care of me even when I don't realize You are doing so. You know what lies ahead, and You are always watching my coming and going. Thank You for Your constant care.

The Battle Is Not Yours

"Our God, will you not judge them? For we have no power to face this vast army that is attacking us. We do not know what to do, but our eyes are on you." . . . Then the Spirit of the LORD came on Jahaziel son of Zechariah. . .as he stood in the assembly. He said: "Listen, King Jehoshaphat and all who live in Judah and Jerusalem! This is what the LORD says to you: 'Do not be afraid or discouraged because of this vast army. For the battle is not yours, but God's. Tomorrow march down against them. . . .You will not have to fight this battle.' "

2 CHRONICLES 20:12, 14–17 NIV

Jehoshaphat and the nation of Judah faced a powerful enemy. They didn't know what to do, but their eyes were on God. If you're in a battle today, where are you looking for help?

....

....

....

....

Are you discouraged by the size of your enemy? Do you trust God to take care of it, or do you feel you need to do something? Ask God for direction in dealing with the problem.

....

....

....

....

....

God expects us to stand strong and put our confidence in Him. That isn't always easy, but the people of Judah had to do just that. God told them to march down against the enemy and take their position against them. Have there been times when God asked you to do something you were afraid to do? How did you handle it?

....

....

....

....

....

God fought for Jehoshaphat and his people, but they had to trust God. How will you trust God to fight for you today?

....

....

....

....

....

Lord, the enemy is coming against me, and I'm afraid. Please help me with this battle. I don't know what to do. I don't know where to turn, but I know that You're able to make a way for me. Help me to get my eyes on You and off the size of the enemy and the battle before me. Help me not to listen to the voices of discouragement around me. Make me strong. When You speak to me, help me to obey. Give me the courage to march out to the battle and take my stand. I know You'll be with me because Your Word tells me so. I need You to fight for me today, Lord.

The Keys of the Kingdom

And I say also unto thee, That thou art Peter, and upon this rock I will build my church; and the gates of hell shall not prevail against it. And I will give unto thee the keys of the kingdom of heaven: and whatsoever thou shalt bind on earth shall be bound in heaven: and whatsoever thou shalt loose on earth shall be loosed in heaven.

MATTHEW 16:18–19 KJV

Jesus promised that the gates of hell would not prevail against His Church. The Church is more than a building; it's people like you who have accepted Christ. You are that Church, and you have been promised victory. How will you claim that promise for yourself?

....

....

....

We have been given the keys of the kingdom of heaven. What purpose do those keys have in the life of a believer? What does this mean to you as a believer?

....

....

....

Jesus said that whatever we bind on earth will be bound in heaven and whatever we loose on earth will be loosed in heaven. What kinds of things would we need to bind or loose on earth? How do we go about doing this?

....

....

If there are things in your life that you need to be loosed from, in your prayer time today, ask God to show you those things that keep you bound, and then ask Him to loose you from those hindrances.

To accomplish the things that Jesus promised us, we need faith. The Bible teaches us that everyone has been given a measure of faith, but what if we don't have the faith needed for this task? Talk to God about it, asking Him to strengthen your faith to do His work.

Jesus, I know I'm a part of Your Church. You promised that the gates of hell would not prevail against it. Make those of us who are believers strong in the faith so Your Church may be strong. Help us not to believe all the voices around us that speak against Your Church. Give us the faith to believe Your words that tell us we can bind things on earth or set free things here on earth and it will be accomplished in heaven as well. Strengthen our faith and help us to stand on Your promises, for Your Word never fails.

A New Heart

*Then will I sprinkle clean water upon you, and ye shall be clean:
from all your filthiness, and from all your idols, will I cleanse you.
A new heart also will I give you, and a new spirit will I put within
you: and I will take away the stony heart out of your flesh, and
I will give you an heart of flesh. And I will put my spirit within
you, and cause you to walk in my statutes, and ye shall keep my
judgments, and do them. And ye shall dwell in the land that I gave
to your fathers; and ye shall be my people, and I will be your God.*
EZEKIEL 36:25–28 KJV

The people of Judah had lived in idolatry for many years. Because
of their sin, they were taken into captivity, but God made them a
promise: He would cleanse them from their sin and their idols. That
promise is for us today also. As you pray, ask God to show you any
idols in your own life that you need to get rid of.

....

....

....

Those things that come between us and God become idols to us
and put us in captivity. If there is something in your life holding you
captive, how can you be free of it?

....

....

....

....

If you feel you need a new heart and a new spirit today, ask God to give them to you.

....

....

....

God said He would take away the stony heart. How does a heart get in this condition?

....

....

....

God will put His Spirit within us so we can walk in His statues and keep His judgments. He knows we can't do this on our own. What is our part in this?

....

....

....

Lord, are there idols in my life that I need to get rid of? Please show me if there are. I don't want anything to come between You and me. Cleanse me from this sin. You promised You would give Your people a new heart and a new spirit. Please give me a heart of flesh and take away the stony heart of resentment, bitterness, and rebellion. Place within me Your Spirit so that I can do those things that please You. Help me to walk in Your statutes every day. Let it become a way of life for me and not one of those when-I-feel-like-it things.

Perfect Peace

Thou wilt keep him in perfect peace, whose mind is stayed on thee: because he trusteth in thee. Trust ye in the LORD for ever: for in the LORD JEHOVAH is everlasting strength. . . . LORD, thou wilt ordain peace for us: for thou also hast wrought all our works in us. . . . If it be possible, as much as lieth in you, live peaceably with all men. . . . Blessed are the peacemakers: for they shall be called the children of God.

ISAIAH 26:3–4, 12; ROMANS 12:18; MATTHEW 5:9 KJV

Current events show us a world in turmoil. It surrounds us. We see it in newspapers, on television, on our computer screens, even on our cell phones. What are some things you can do to keep the negative reports from influencing your life?

....

....

....

How can we have peace when everyone around us seems bent on causing unrest?

....

....

....

As Christians, should we get involved in politics and world events? Why or why not?

....

....

....

God promises to keep us in perfect peace if our minds are stayed on Him. How can you keep your mind on God when there are so many demands on your life every day?

....

....

....

"In the Lord Jehovah is everlasting strength." How do we obtain this strength for ourselves?

....

....

....

We're instructed to live peaceably with all people if possible. Pray today for those people in your life that you find it hard to be at peace with. What causes the unrest? Is there something you can do to make peace?

....

....

....

God, some days the chaos that surrounds our world presses in on me. I know I can't do anything about the world situation. That's in Your hands. But it keeps me troubled in my own spirit. You said in Your Word that if we keep our minds on You, You'll keep us in perfect peace. I need that peace today. Help me to place my trust in You and accept the peace You have for me. Help me not to allow the negative reports I hear to keep me from having Your peace in my life. You know also that I have my own battles to fight with people who rub me the wrong way. I need to find a way to make peace with them. Help me to be a peacemaker.

Chief or Servant?

*But to sit on my right hand and on my left hand is not mine
to give; but it shall be given to them for whom it is prepared.
And when the ten heard it, they began to be much displeased
with James and John. But Jesus called them to him, and saith
unto them, Ye know that they which are accounted to rule over
the Gentiles exercise lordship over them; and their great ones
exercise authority upon them. But so shall it not be among you:
but whosoever will be great among you, shall be your minister:
and whosoever of you will be the chiefest, shall be servant of
all. For even the Son of man came not to be ministered unto,
but to minister, and to give his life a ransom for many.*

MARK 10:40–45 KJV

To some, success means having a certain position with power and
authority. If we find ourselves in a position of authority, what should
our conduct be? What should be the Christian's view of power? If
you're having trouble in this area, ask God to give you wisdom.

....

....

....

Jesus said those who wanted to be the chiefest would be the servant of all. What does it mean to be a servant or to have a servant's
heart? How does this fit into your plans? As you pray, ask God to
show you where He wants you to serve.

....

....

....

....

....

....

Jesus said that He came to minister to others. If we're to follow His example, we must minister to those around us. Do you find it hard to serve others? Why or why not?

....

....

....

....

....

....

Lord, I know Your idea of success is different from mine, so help me know Your definition of success for my life and help me be content to serve wherever You place me. Show me what it means to have a servant's heart, and place that spirit within me. Teach me to be more like You, who came to serve. I pray today for those in authority over me that they will make good decisions for everyone concerned and that they will use their power for good and not evil. Help me to make the right decisions concerning those I'm involved with. Help me to put others' needs before my own and serve with a servant's heart.

The Lord Is My Shepherd

The Lord is my shepherd, I lack nothing. He makes me lie down in green pastures, he leads me beside quiet waters, he refreshes my soul. He guides me along the right paths for his name's sake. Even though I walk through the darkest valley, I will fear no evil, for you are with me; your rod and your staff, they comfort me. You prepare a table before me in the presence of my enemies. You anoint my head with oil; my cup overflows. Surely your goodness and love will follow me all the days of my life, and I will dwell in the house of the Lord forever.

PSALM 23:1–6 NIV

A shepherd leads and directs his sheep, feeds them and keeps them safe. In what area of your life do you need direction? If you have a special need today, this psalm tells us that the Lord is our Shepherd and we lack nothing. In your prayer time, talk to the Lord about your needs. Ask Him to lead you today.

....

....

....

....

If you're feeling stressed and need some quiet time, ask Jesus to show you the quiet waters and green pastures He has for you. Let Him refresh you as you spend time in prayer with Him.

....

....

....

....

What are the questions about your future that cloud your mind? As you pray, ask God to guide you. When He walks with us, we can live without fear of the future.

....

....

....

God's anointing restores and heals us. How do you want Him to anoint you today?

....

....

....

What are some of the ways you're experiencing God's goodness and love in your life? Give Him thanks for those things when you pray.

....

....

....

Lord, I need direction today. With You as my Shepherd, I know I have everything I need, but sometimes I forget that when problems come my way. Help me to rely on You. Restore and refresh me with Your Spirit. Lead me to that place in You where I can experience green pastures and quiet waters in my life. Whenever I'm afraid, help me to remember that You're always with me, guiding and comforting me. Anoint me as only You can so that my cup overflows, spilling over onto others. Help me to acknowledge and appreciate Your goodness and love in my life.

Willing and Obedient

Wash and make yourselves clean. Take your evil deeds out of my sight; stop doing wrong. Learn to do right; seek justice. Defend the oppressed. Take up the cause of the fatherless; plead the case of the widow. "Come now, let us settle the matter," says the LORD. "Though your sins are like scarlet, they shall be as white as snow; though they are red as crimson, they shall be like wool. If you are willing and obedient, you will eat the good things of the land; but if you resist and rebel, you will be devoured by the sword."

ISAIAH 1:16–20 NIV

How do we wash and make ourselves clean before God? If you feel the need to do this in your own life, pray about it, asking God to show you the things to delete from your life.

....

....

....

....

People have different ideas about what is right or wrong. This scripture passage tells us to learn to do right. How can we know when something is wrong for us? Where should you go for help or direction in making your decisions?

....

....

....

....

These verses encourage us to defend the oppressed and to help the fatherless and widows. Do you know of some who might need your help? What kind of help should we give those around us? How far should we go? Make a list of those people, and during your prayer time, ask God for opportunities to minister to them.

....

....

....

God is looking for those who are willing and obedient. Pray about your attitude toward God's plans for your life, asking Him to make you an obedient servant.

....

....

....

What does it mean to "eat the good things of the land"? Is it a spiritual promise or a physical one?

....

....

....

Lord, You know there are things in my life that aren't right. I don't feel clean. Forgive me for the sin in my life. Help me to stop doing wrong and to learn to do right. Help my life to please You. I know there are those around me who need someone to care about them and help them. Lead me to those people. Give me the courage to defend them and lead them to You. Give me a willing heart. Remove any rebellion in my life and make me an obedient servant.

Choose Life

I call heaven and earth to record this day against you,
that I have set before you life and death, blessing and cursing:
therefore choose life, that both thou and thy seed may live:
that thou mayest love the LORD thy God, and that thou mayest
obey his voice, and that thou mayest cleave unto him: for he
is thy life, and the length of thy days: that thou mayest
dwell in the land which the LORD sware unto thy fathers,
to Abraham, to Isaac, and to Jacob, to give them.
DEUTERONOMY 30:19–20 KJV

What future plans are you making for yourself or your family? How can you know which plans are right?

....

....

....

....

If you're worried about the future, talk to God about your plans; then listen for His direction. It might help to write down your plans and pray over the list, asking God to help you eliminate those things that can steer you wrong.

....

....

....

....

How our lives turn out is due to the decisions we make and the paths we choose to follow. If you've made wrong decisions in the past, ask God for wisdom in future decisions. When He speaks to you, trust that He knows what's best for you.

....

....

....

God calls us to choose life and blessings. This requires obedience on our part to experience these blessings. What are some blessings you've already experienced?

....

....

....

Focus on holding fast to God, choosing the life He has promised, and allow Him to be a part of your plans for the future.

....

....

....

Jesus, You know the plans I've been making and whether they're the right ones. Sometimes I get the silly notion that I know what's best for my life. You and I both know that I don't. I want to make good decisions for the future. In the past, I've made some mistakes, but I don't want to repeat them. I want to choose life and blessings for me and my family. Thank You for the blessings You've already given me. I know You have greater things in store for me if I obey Your voice. Make me sensitive to Your voice so I can know which direction to take. Help me be obedient, trust You, and hold fast to Your hand.

Watch What You Say

*For out of the abundance of the heart the mouth speaketh.
A good man out of the good treasure of the heart bringeth forth
good things: and an evil man out of the evil treasure bringeth
forth evil things. But I say unto you, That every idle word that
men shall speak, they shall give account thereof in the day
of judgment. For by thy words thou shalt be justified,
and by thy words thou shalt be condemned. . . . Be not
deceived: evil communications corrupt good manners.*

Matthew 12:34–37; 1 Corinthians 15:33 kjv

Sometimes we speak before we think. Once words are spoken, they can't be taken back. What are some words you've spoken that you wish you could take back? If it involved others, what can you do to correct the situation?

....

....

....

....

If you sometimes speak before you think, what can you do to change this habit? If you have asked God and others to forgive your hasty words, you need to forgive yourself and move on. You've done all you can do to repair the damage.

....

....

....

....

In this scripture passage, Jesus says that what we speak comes from the heart. What does your speech say about the condition of your heart?

....

....

....

Not only can the words we speak do harm, but the words we listen to from others can be harmful also. How can you respond to someone who wants to gossip?

....

....

....

Our words either justify us or condemn us. If you're concerned about the words you use or how you talk, spend time in prayer asking God to make your words edifying to those around you.

....

....

....

Lord, You know I sometimes speak without thinking. I've been guilty of sticking my foot in my mouth too often. I've probably offended others with my careless words. Please forgive me and give me the courage to make it right with those I've hurt. Teach me how to change this habit. Help me to live in such a way that my heart will be filled with good things, and when I speak those are the words that come out. Show me how to make my speech a blessing to those around me. Keep me from speaking only idle words, and help me not to allow evil communications to corrupt my manners.

Make a Joyful Noise

O come, let us sing unto the Lord: let us make a joyful noise to the rock of our salvation. . . . Make a joyful noise unto the Lord, all ye lands. Serve the Lord with gladness: come before his presence with singing. Know ye that the Lord he is God: it is he that hath made us, and not we ourselves; we are his people, and the sheep of his pasture. Enter into his gates with thanksgiving, and into his courts with praise: be thankful unto him, and bless his name. For the Lord is good; his mercy is everlasting; and his truth endureth to all generations.
PSALM 95:1; 100:1–5 KJV

Praise is a natural response to answered prayers, but answered prayer shouldn't be the only time we give God praise. What are some other times we can offer praise to God?

....

....

....

....

If our time with God is spent asking for things, we will miss out on a vital part of communication with Him. He wants to hear our praises. How can praise be a part of your prayer time?

....

....

....

....

....

It's important to recognize who God is when we pray. What are some ways you acknowledge Him in your prayers?

....

....

....

This psalm encourages us to enter into the Lord's gates with thanksgiving. It's more than just showing up for church services; it's entering into His presence in a spirit of thanks. How can you enter these gates during your personal prayer time?

....

....

....

Your time with God is personal, just you and Him. Challenge yourself to do more than tell Him about your needs when you pray. Spend time singing, acknowledging His presence, expressing your love for Him, and thanking Him for His goodness.

....

....

....

I love You, Lord. I want to praise and worship You today. Sometimes I'm busy asking You to do things for me. Today, I just want to worship You. You're worthy of all praise. All honor and glory belong to You. You're my Creator, my Shepherd, and my sovereign God. I'm thankful for Your presence in my life. You're always there when I need You. Thank You for caring about me. You have extended mercy to me and given me so many blessings. I'm thankful for the truth You have given me. I worship You in all Your glory.

I Am with Thee

*"I took you from the ends of the earth, from its farthest corners
I called you. I said, 'You are my servant'; I have chosen you and
have not rejected you. So do not fear, for I am with you; do not
be dismayed, for I am your God. I will strengthen you and
help you; I will uphold you with my righteous right hand. . . .
For I am the L<small>ORD</small> your God who takes hold of your right
hand and says to you, Do not fear; I will help you."*
ISAIAH 41:9–10, 13 NIV

God has called each person to follow Him and be His servant. He
has chosen you, but how do you know you are chosen? What are
some ways you are answering the call?

....

....

....

What are some things you or someone in your family are dismayed
about? Talk to God about those things that cause fear and dismay.
Don't try to carry these burdens alone.

....

....

....

God has promised to be present with you, to strengthen and help
you. If you are feeling uncertain, spend time claiming His promise
to be with you as you pray.

....

....

Satan doesn't want us to feel confident in God. He tries to make us doubt God's promises. He attempts to get our thoughts focused on everything around us instead of on God. Do whatever it takes to keep your mind on God. Focus your thoughts on His Word. Sing a praise chorus as you go about your day, thanking God for what He has done.

Fear can temporarily make us forget God's promises. Pray about your fear. Spend time talking to God and asking Him for faith to believe His promises and to believe He is holding your hand.

Father, Your Word tells me I have been chosen by You to be Your servant. Sometimes I feel unworthy to be Your servant. Thank You for choosing me anyway. Show me how to serve You. Sometimes fear gets in the way of my following You. I allow circumstances around me to fog my thinking. Satan tries to make me doubt Your Word. Strengthen me and help me to realize You're beside me, holding my hand through all my problems. Increase my faith to believe in Your power to protect and shield me.

Love Not the World

Love not the world, neither the things that are in the world.
If any man love the world, the love of the Father is not in him.
For all that is in the world, the lust of the flesh, and the lust of
the eyes, and the pride of life, is not of the Father, but is of
the world. And the world passeth away, and the lust thereof:
but he that doeth the will of God abideth forever. . . . And now,
little children, abide in him; that, when he shall appear, we may
have confidence, and not be ashamed before him at his coming.
1 John 2:15–17, 28 kjv

We're a part of the world we live in. We don't know any other life but this one. The world holds many attractive pleasures. How do we keep from loving the world and the things in the world? Where do we draw the line?

....

....

....

....

We're taught that if we love this world, the love of the Father isn't in us. How do we keep God first in our lives?

....

....

....

....

This life is temporary. Everything we have here will pass away someday. Only God's plans will last. He holds the future in His hands. How does this affect your decision to acquire possessions?

....

....

....

The pull of worldly possessions and pleasures can be very strong. Ask God to direct you in making decisions about your life and what you become involved in.

....

....

....

If we abide in Christ, we can have confidence at His coming and not be afraid to face Him. How do we abide in Christ while still living here on earth so we can have this confidence?

....

....

....

God, I know that You have given us many wonderful things to enjoy. There are so many things that look good in this world. Yet I know that as Your child, I can't indulge every desire that I feel. Help me not to love this world so much that it shuts out my love for You. When lust creeps up on me and the pride of life tries to draw me into the wrong thing, give me strength to resist those temptations. Fill me with Your love so that all those things around me fall away and become less important. Help me to be able to stand before You when the time comes and not be ashamed of my life.

Living Epistles

Are we beginning to commend ourselves again? Or do we need, like some people, letters of recommendation to you or from you? You yourselves are our letter, written on our hearts, known and read by everyone. You show that you are a letter from Christ, the result of our ministry, written not with ink but with the Spirit of the living God, not on tablets of stone but on tablets of human hearts. Such confidence we have through Christ before God. Not that we are competent in ourselves to claim anything for ourselves, but our competence comes from God. He has made us competent as ministers of a new covenant—not of the letter but of the Spirit; for the letter kills, but the Spirit gives life.

2 CORINTHIANS 3:1-6 NIV

Christians are letters to the world, not written with pen and ink by man's hand, but written by God's Spirit. What kind of letter do people read when they see your life?

....

....

....

....

Our hearts are the tablet that the letter is written on. This letter is the good news of Jesus Christ. In your prayer time, ask God to examine your heart and make the letter clear for others to see.

....

....

....

....

We can do nothing in ourselves. We must have God's help to minister to others. Ask God for His direction in your work for Him.

....

....

....

Sometimes we try to handle situations on our own, forgetting that God wants us to rely on Him. How can we keep from thinking we are self-sufficient?

....

....

....

How can we become more effective letters to the world around us?

....

....

....

Jesus, examine my heart and write Your letter there so others may see You in me. Wash away all the things that make the letter blurry and hard to read. Don't allow my letter to fade with time, but make it plain, keep it clear. I need Your help in my efforts to be a witnessing letter to others. In the past, I've tried to do things on my own, but without You I'm helpless. Help me to put my confidence in You and not in my own abilities. Help me not to be so self-sufficient, relying on my knowledge, but help me to study Your Word and learn from You. Teach me how to be a minister of the new covenant of the Spirit.

Justified through Faith

Therefore, since we have been justified through faith, we have peace with God through our Lord Jesus Christ, through whom we have gained access by faith into this grace in which we now stand. And we boast in the hope of the glory of God. Not only so, but we also glory in our sufferings, because we know that suffering produces perseverance; perseverance, character; and character, hope. And hope does not put us to shame, because God's love has been poured out into our hearts through the Holy Spirit, who has been given to us. You see, at just the right time, when we were still powerless, Christ died for the ungodly. Very rarely will anyone die for a righteous person, though for a good person someone might possibly dare to die. But God demonstrates his own love for us in this: While we were still sinners, Christ died for us.

ROMANS 5:1–8 NIV

What are you troubled about today? Talk to Jesus about it and claim peace for yourself.

....

....

....

You may find it hard to glory in suffering. It's not always easy to give praise when you're hurting. Challenge yourself to give God praise at all times. Ask Him for the strength to do so.

....

....

....

Suffering produces other characteristics in our lives as listed in verses 3 and 4. What are some characteristics God has developed in your life?

....

....

....

We have hope because God's love has been poured into our hearts through the Holy Spirit. What are some ways you're experiencing this hope?

....

....

....

Even when we were unworthy of His love, Christ died for us. In your prayer time, express your love to Him for what He did on the cross.

....

....

....

Jesus, I'm troubled about some things today. I can't seem to think about anything except what's bothering me. You know what those things are and how I cannot find peace because of them. I can't do anything about these troubles. Help me surrender them to You, and give me peace about them. Help me to praise and thank You even in the middle of my troubles and pain, even though I might not feel like doing so. I have so much to thank You for. You loved me when I was unlovable and died for me when I didn't deserve it. Thank You for Your great love and the hope I have because of that love.

Pulling Down Strongholds

For though we walk in the flesh, we do not war after the flesh:
(for the weapons of our warfare are not carnal, but mighty
through God to the pulling down of strongholds;) casting down
imaginations, and every high thing that exalteth itself against the
knowledge of God, and bringing into captivity every thought to
the obedience of Christ; and having in a readiness to revenge
all disobedience, when your obedience is fulfilled.

2 CORINTHIANS 10:3–6 KJV

What strongholds do you need to tear down in your life? When you pray, tell God about each one of them, asking for His help.

....

....

....

....

In our natural minds, it's hard to grasp the love of Christ. It's greater than any earthly knowledge we might obtain. Even though you can't grasp its depth, ask God for more of His love.

....

....

....

....

If you're in a spiritual battle, remember that God has given you the spiritual weapons you need to fight against the flesh to pull down those strongholds in your life. What are the weapons we use in spiritual battles? In prayer, ask God for the strength to use the weapons He has given you.

....

....

....

How can you control your imagination and bring your thoughts into captivity? Thoughts may flit through our minds, but we don't have to dwell on them.

....

....

....

Ask God to open your spiritual eyes so you can identify those things that exalt themselves against the knowledge of God.

....

....

....

Lord, I'm having a hard time fighting desires that I know are wrong. I can't defeat them by myself. Even though the desires are present with me in my physical life, I know this is a spiritual battle. I need Your help to pull down these strongholds. Help me to control my imagination and those thoughts that aren't pleasing to You. I'm so ashamed to have thoughts that aren't right, but sometimes they run wild and I can't seem to control them. Give me a pure mind and help me to think on things that are pleasing to You. Open my spiritual eyes to see those things that, although they might seem harmless to me, the enemy is using against me. Show me what I need to do.

Success in Life

"For I know the plans I have for you" declares the LORD, "plans to prosper you and not to harm you, plans to give you hope and a future. Then you will call on me and come and pray to me, and I will listen to you. You will seek me and find me when you seek me with all your heart. I will be found by you," declares the LORD, "and will bring you back from captivity. I will gather you from all the nations and places where I have banished you," declares the LORD, "and will bring you back to the place from which I carried you into exile."
JEREMIAH 29:11–14 NIV

Most people want to be successful in something. It may be getting an education, finding the right job, or raising their family or finances. What things do you want to be successful in?

....

....

....

....

If you want to succeed, spend time in prayer asking God what His plans are for you.

....

....

....

....

Sometimes we get into trouble because we think we know best, but only God knows the future, and He wants to give you hope for that time. As you seek God in prayer, ask Him to order your future.

....

....

....

We find the Lord when we seek Him with all our heart. How do we seek Him with our whole heart?

....

....

....

The Lord declared He would restore Israel. They had gone their own way and ended up in captivity, but His mercy would lead them back and restore what they had lost. If you have lost something because of a bad decision, ask God for restoration.

....

....

....

Lord, I thank You for the promises in Your Word. I need help planning for the future. I don't want to make mistakes and end up in trouble. I know that You have plans for me and hope for the future. Show me the plans You have for my life. Order my steps each day and help me to make wise decisions. Help me to follow You and listen for Your voice in every situation. I've made some mistakes in the past. Forgive me for not seeking You before I acted. Restore me to the place You have for me, and help me to seek You with all my heart so I can succeed as You want me to.

God's Word Gives Light

Thy testimonies are wonderful: therefore doth my soul keep them. The entrance of thy words giveth light; it giveth understanding unto the simple. I opened my mouth, and panted: for I longed for thy commandments. Look thou upon me, and be merciful unto me, as thou usest to do unto those that love thy name. Order my steps in thy word: and let not any iniquity have dominion over me. Deliver me from the oppression of man: so will I keep thy precepts. Make thy face to shine upon thy servant; and teach me thy statutes. Rivers of waters run down mine eyes, because they keep not thy law.

PSALM 119:129–36 KJV

God's Word brings light and understanding into our lives as we read it. The more we read, the more it becomes familiar to us. How often do you read the Bible?

....

....

....

The Bible is full of testimonies and stories that encourage us in our Christian walk. If you need encouragement today, read God's Word, asking God to open your understanding as you read.

....

....

....

What are you doing to learn more about the Bible?

....

....

When we don't understand something about God's commandments or statutes, we can ask Him to open our understanding as we read His Word. When you have a question, take it to God in prayer and ask Him for His help.

....

....

....

As you read God's Word, ask Him to order your steps in His Word and to help you keep His precepts so that His words become a part of your daily life.

....

....

....

Pray for others that they might have a hunger for more of God's Word.

....

....

....

Lord, thank You for the Bible, Your Word, that encourages us and tells us how to live each day. Give me a greater desire to know more about it. Help me to read and study the Bible more often, and give me understanding as I read. Give me a longing for more of You. Let Your Word become such a big part of my life that I want more and more. Order my steps in Your Word so that I can live a clean life before You. Let the wisdom in Your Word influence my thinking and my decisions.

You Are Salt

"You are the salt of the earth. But if the salt loses its saltiness, how can it be made salty again? It is no longer good for anything, except to be thrown out and trampled underfoot. You are the light of the world. A town built on a hill cannot be hidden. Neither do people light a lamp and put it under a bowl. Instead they put it on its stand, and it gives light to everyone in the house. In the same way, let your light shine before others, that they may see your good deeds and glorify your Father in heaven."

MATTHEW 5:13–16 NIV

Jesus said, "You are the salt of the earth." What makes you the salt of the earth? Are there things you do that qualify you for this characteristic?

....

....

....

....

When we lose our saltiness, how can we be restored to our original state? Spend time in prayer if you're in doubt about your own condition of saltiness.

....

....

....

....

In the same way that we are salt, we are also light to the world around us. In what way are you salt and light to those around you?

Ask God to show you those who need to be influenced by salt and light.

....

....

....

....

....

Because we are human, sometimes our light doesn't burn as brightly as it should. If there are times when you feel your light has dimmed, spend time talking to God about it. How can your light shine so that it glorifies the Father in heaven and not you?

....

....

....

....

....

Jesus, You said we are the salt of the earth and a light to the world. Sometimes my light grows dim and my salt isn't too salty. Forgive me for allowing that to happen. I want to be salt and light to those around me. Give me the saltiness I need so I can flavor other people's lives with Your love. Help me not to hide my light from those who need to see it, even those who may tick me off sometimes and especially those who don't care for me. As I work for You, let others see You and not me through the deeds that I do. Let the work that I do bring glory to You so others may glorify You.

Love Your Enemies

"But to you who are listening I say: Love your enemies, do good to those who hate you, bless those who curse you, pray for those who mistreat you. If someone slaps you on one cheek, turn to them the other also. If someone takes your coat, do not withhold your shirt from them. Give to everyone who asks you, and if anyone takes what belongs to you, do not demand it back. Do to others as you would have them do to you. If you love those who love you, what credit is that to you? Even sinners love those who love them. . . . But love your enemies, do good to them, and lend to them without expecting to get anything back."

LUKE 6:27–32, 35 NIV

What kind of emotions are you feeling today because of someone else's actions? How has it affected your treatment of that person?

....

....

....

If you feel there are people who are your enemies, pray for them, asking God to bless them.

....

....

....

If you have a hard time praying for those who mistreat you, ask God to help you love them as He wants you to.

....

....

....

....

Sometimes we feel justified in our feelings of anger or resentment toward people who have treated us badly. Often the hurt is so deep we can't be objective in our thinking. Ask God to help you get rid of those feelings and better understand the situation.

....

....

....

....

In your prayer time, ask God to give you a heart to do good to others despite how they may act.

....

....

....

....

Lord, there are some people I have a hard time getting along with. In fact, I don't even want to be around them. I know You're not pleased with that attitude. Forgive me and help me to pray for them in spite of how they act. I know I'm not perfect either. Bless them, Lord, so they can see Your love at work in their lives. Take away the hurt that keeps me so full of resentment and anger for the way I've been treated. Help me to look past my pain and see the situation for what it is. Help me forgive them even if they don't ask me to. Fill my heart with love for these people, and help me to do good to them even when they abuse me.

Living Water

Jesus answered and said unto her, If thou knewest the gift of God, and who it is that saith to thee, Give me to drink; thou wouldest have asked of him, and he would have given thee living water. The woman saith unto him, Sir, thou hast nothing to draw with, and the well is deep: from whence then hast thou that living water? Art thou greater than our father Jacob, which gave us the well, and drank thereof himself, and his children, and his cattle? Jesus answered and said unto her, Whosoever drinketh of this water shall thirst again: but whosoever drinketh of the water that I shall give him shall never thirst; but the water that I shall give him shall be in him a well of water springing up into everlasting life.

JOHN 4:10–14 KJV

The woman at the well could see only in the natural. From her perspective, the well was deep and Jesus had no way of drawing the water. What problem are you facing today? Ask God to open your eyes to see what He can do in your situation.

....

....

....

Jesus said we would never thirst again if we drink of the water He offers. What does He mean that we will never thirst again?

....

....

....

....

Sometimes earthly wells run dry, but this one is eternal. What does this mean to you when you drink of this water?

....

....

....

The last verse says it will be "a well of water springing up into everlasting life." If you have experienced these springs of living water, how can it help you deal with today's problem?

....

....

....

Jesus shared His living water with the woman at the well. Ask God to show you someone to share this water with.

....

....

....

Lord, open my spiritual eyes so that I can see what is possible with You. I desire this living water in my life. You said whoever drinks this water would never thirst again. That means me, doesn't it? I want to experience that refreshing that never dies. Let me be filled with this living water so I will never be thirsty again. Let this water spring up, giving me hope for the future, for eternal life, and overflow to others. Don't let my well ever run dry. Help me to stay in the place where the water is always flowing.

Intercession by the Spirit

*For in this hope we were saved. But hope that is seen is no hope
at all. Who hopes for what they already have? But if we hope for
what we do not yet have, we wait for it patiently. In the same way,
the Spirit helps us in our weakness. We do not know what we
ought to pray for, but the Spirit himself intercedes for us through
wordless groans. And he who searches our hearts knows the
mind of the Spirit, because the Spirit intercedes for God's
people in accordance with the will of God. And we know
that in all things God works for the good of those who
love him, who have been called according to his purpose.*

ROMANS 8:24–28 NIV

If our hope is built in Christ, we are saved through Him. What is
your hope built on?

....

....

....

....

What are the weaknesses in your life that you need help with?
Spend time talking to God about those weaknesses. He cares what
you're feeling today.

....

....

....

....

....

Sometimes we can't find the words we need to express what we're feeling. We may not even know what to pray for. How can we allow the Holy Spirit to intercede for us as we pray?

....

....

....

God searches our hearts and knows the Spirit. They work together. The Spirit intercedes for us. He knows exactly what we are feeling and what we need. As you pray, trust the Father, Jesus, and the Holy Spirit to work out your problems.

....

....

....

The Holy Spirit works according to God's will, not ours. If you believe that God is working for your good, take time to commit any questions or weaknesses to Him.

....

....

....

Jesus, help me not to place my hope in people or possessions. I have hope in You. I know that the Spirit helps me in my weak times. I don't always know how to pray about situations or even what to pray for sometimes, but Your Word tells me that the Spirit Himself intercedes for me. I don't even have to speak words. He understands my groaning and crying when I can't seem to express myself any other way. Help me to yield myself and my problems to You as You search my heart, knowing that the Spirit is interceding for me according to Your will and that You will work everything out for my good.

A Living Sacrifice

I beseech you therefore, brethren, by the mercies of God, that ye present your bodies a living sacrifice, holy, acceptable unto God, which is your reasonable service. And be not conformed to this world: but be ye transformed by the renewing of your mind, that ye may prove what is that good, and acceptable, and perfect, will of God. For I say, through the grace given unto me, to every man that is among you, not to think of himself more highly than he ought to think; but to think soberly, according as God hath dealt to every man the measure of faith.

ROMANS 12:1–3 KJV

To be acceptable to God, we must be willing to put ourselves on the altar of sacrifice. Paul wrote that this is not an unreasonable request; this is our reasonable service to God. What does this mean to you personally? What needs to happen in your life to present yourself as a living sacrifice?

....

....

....

....

What kinds of things might keep you from presenting your body as a living sacrifice to God? How can you change those things?

....

....

....

....

We can be transformed by the renewing of our minds. This enables us to know the perfect will of God. If you need this transformation, ask God to renew your mind.

....

....

....

Christ has extended grace to each of us. We cannot transform ourselves. We must have His help. Ask Christ for more of His grace in your life.

....

....

....

As you pray, ask God to transform you into the living sacrifice He wants you to become.

....

....

....

God, You know me better than I know myself. I want to be pleasing and acceptable to You, but sometimes it's hard to put myself on the altar and sacrifice my will to You. Remove those things in my life that keep me from being holy and acceptable to You. Show me where I've allowed myself to conform to the world, and transform me. Renew my mind. Change my thinking so I can know Your will for me instead of just plunging through life doing my own thing. Help me not to think more of myself than I should. If it were not for Your grace, I would be nothing. Give me the faith I need to believe that You're working out all things for my good.

Live the Right Way

*Blessed is the one who does not walk in step with the wicked
or stand in the way that sinners take or sit in the company of
mockers, but whose delight is in the law of the Lord, and who
meditates on his law day and night. That person is like a tree
planted by streams of water, which yields its fruit in season
and whose leaf does not wither—whatever they do prospers.
Not so the wicked! They are like chaff that the wind blows away.
Therefore the wicked will not stand in the judgment, nor sinners in
the assembly of the righteous. For the Lord watches over the way
of the righteous, but the way of the wicked leads to destruction.*

PSALM 1:1–6 NIV

What are you delighting in today and how is it influencing your
daily life? Who is influencing your thoughts and decisions?

....

....

....

....

If we allow ourselves to be influenced by the world, we will miss out
on God's blessings. He wants us to avoid the ways of the wicked
and spend time living according to His Word. In your prayer time,
talk to God about who and what influences you.

....

....

....

....

How can you be like a tree planted by the water whose leaf doesn't wither? This psalm tells us that when we delight in the Lord and meditate on His law, we will prosper. What are some things you might need to pray about so you can be like a fruitful tree?

....

....

....

The tree mentioned in today's verses is planted by streams of water. As Christians, we need spiritual water to grow and develop. Where does this water come from?

....

....

....

Commit your daily walk to God. He is watching over the way of the righteous.

....

....

....

Lord, are there some things in my life that I need to remove? If so, forgive me and help me to avoid those things that influence me in the wrong way. Take away those desires that would put me in the wrong kind of company. Help me to delight in Your law and spend time reading and meditating on Your Word. Show me how to conduct my life on a daily basis. I want to be like a fruitful tree that pleases You and prospers. I know You are watching over me and will keep me from taking the wrong path.

Put On the New Woman

If ye then be risen with Christ, seek those things which are above, where Christ sitteth on the right hand of God. Set your affection on things above, not on things on the earth. For ye are dead, and your life is hid with Christ in God. . . . Mortify therefore your members which are upon the earth; fornication, uncleanness, inordinate affection, evil concupiscence, and covetousness, which is idolatry. . . . But now ye also put off all these; anger, wrath, malice, blasphemy, filthy communication out of your mouth. Lie not one to another, seeing that ye have put off the old man with his deeds; and have put on the new man, which is renewed in knowledge after the image of him that created him.

COLOSSIANS 3:1–3, 5, 8–10 KJV

As Christians, we are risen with Christ. We are to seek after and set our affection on things above, not earthly things. Where does your affection lie?

....

....

....

....

What does it mean that "your life is hid with Christ in God"?

....

....

....

....

....

Sometimes people think some sins are much worse than others. Because of this, we may overlook something displeasing to God. Ask God to show you if there is something in your life that displeases Him.

....

....

....

Paul wrote to the Colossians about the importance of getting rid of unclean actions like fornication and covetousness, but he also pointed out anger, filthy talk, and lying. The world accepts these actions as normal. How do you feel about them?

....

....

....

When we accept Christ, we leave the old life behind. Sometimes Satan tries to bring up the past. If you're troubled by something from the past, ask God to help you set your affection on Him and not the past.

....

....

....

Jesus, thank You for the life You've given me. Help me to set my affection on You and what You want me to be. Show me if there is something in my life that is displeasing to You. Give me the power to get rid of anything in my life that is unclean. Center my desires on pleasing You. Help me to control my emotions so that I'm not saying or doing something wrong. You've forgiven me and made me a new person. Help me not to dwell on the past, but live as a new person in Christ.

Mind Your Own Business

Now about your love for one another we do not need to write to you, for you yourselves have been taught by God to love each other. And in fact, you do love all of God's family throughout Macedonia. Yet we urge you, brothers and sisters, to do so more and more, and to make it your ambition to lead a quiet life: You should mind your own business and work with your hands, just as we told you, so that your daily life may win the respect of outsiders and so that you will not be dependent on anybody.

1 Thessalonians 4:9–12 niv

We're taught to love one another, but sometimes there are people we find hard to love. Pray for those people, asking God to bless them and to help you love them through His love for you.

....

....

....

....

How do we lead a quiet life when the world around us moves at a hectic pace? Are there things you can do to create a quiet atmosphere in your home?

....

....

....

....

Sometimes it's hard to mind our own business, especially if it involves someone we know or love. How can we mind our own business and not be the neighborhood busybody or participate in gossip?

....

....

....

As Christians, we should live in a way that pleases Christ and draws people's attention to Him. As those around us watch us walk through life, go about our jobs, and raise our families, what should our conduct be?

....

....

....

In your prayer time, ask God to help you live in such a way that He will be glorified and others can see Christ in you.

....

....

....

God, help me to love those I'm having a hard time with. You know who they are. Fill me with more of Your love so I can love them through You. I can't seem to do it alone. Help me not to stir up trouble by contributing to gossip or taking sides against someone else. Show me how to live a quiet life and mind my own business. Help me not to be a busybody, getting involved in something I shouldn't. Show me how to take care of my own home and family and set an example for others to follow. Help me to live in such a way that other people will see You in my life.

Be Not Troubled

Concerning the coming of our Lord Jesus Christ and our being gathered to him, we ask you, brothers and sisters, not to become easily unsettled or alarmed by the teaching allegedly from us—whether by a prophecy or by word of mouth or by letter— asserting that the day of the Lord has already come. Don't let anyone deceive you in any way, for that day will not come until the rebellion occurs and the man of lawlessness is revealed, the man doomed to destruction. He will oppose and will exalt himself over everything that is called God or is worshiped, so that he sets himself up in God's temple, proclaiming himself to be God.

2 Thessalonians 2:1–4 NIV

What troubles you about future events in our world? Talk to God about your worries. Sometimes we forget He's in control. When we remember this, it goes a long way toward keeping us more settled as we face each day and less troubled when we see or hear negative things.

....

....

....

If you believe that Christ is coming again, what should be your biggest concern?

....

....

....

Many prophetic voices are being heard today, but not all of them are speaking the truth. We can't allow ourselves to be deceived by the wrong message. What can you do to be sure you're listening to the right voice?

....

....

....

Paul told the Thessalonians not to be unsettled or alarmed by the wrong message. What are some ways you can stay calm and keep your mind centered on Christ and His peace?

....

....

....

Ask God to direct your mind and thoughts about world events. As you seek Him, take time to be quiet in His presence and to listen for His voice.

....

....

....

Lord, I believe You're coming again, and I want to be ready to meet You. I hear a lot of talk and many people expressing their views about the end times. Sometimes they contradict each other, which is confusing. Help me to know who is speaking Your truth. Don't let me be deceived by anyone. Keep me calm in the face of all that's happening around me, and help me not to become shaken in my faith. Strengthen my confidence and faith in You. Help me to remember that You are in control. Give me the stability I need to stay true to You and Your Word.

A Workman Approved

Do your best to present yourself to God as one approved, a worker who does not need to be ashamed and who correctly handles the word of truth. Avoid godless chatter, because those who indulge in it will become more and more ungodly. Their teaching will spread like gangrene. Among them are Hymenaeus and Philetus, who have departed from the truth. They say that the resurrection has already taken place, and they destroy the faith of some. Nevertheless, God's solid foundation stands firm, sealed with this inscription: "The Lord knows those who are his" and, "Everyone who confesses the name of the Lord must turn away from wickedness."

2 Timothy 2:15–19 NIV

Presenting yourself to God as an approved worker could include places such as your home, your job, or the church. In what way are you striving to be a worker who is pleasing to God?

....

....

....

....

People sometimes discredit God's Word. What does it mean to handle the word of truth correctly?

....

....

....

....

In this age of technology, we can connect with people around the world. It's easy to get caught up in what Paul called "godless chatter." If you feel you've participated in godless chatter, pray about it, asking God to forgive you and use the words of your mouth for His glory.

It's important to know God's Word and what it says so we can distinguish between the truth and false information. As you read, ask God to open your understanding of His truth.

If we belong to the Lord and confess His name, we must turn away from those things we know to be wrong. Ask God to give you strength to avoid evil.

God, I want to please You in all I do. I want to be an approved worker so I won't be ashamed of my life. Help me to conduct myself in such a way that those around me will see You in me as I work for the kingdom. Let my conversation be truthful, and help me to handle Your Word with great care so I won't mislead anyone. Help me to avoid godless chatter. Let the Holy Spirit speak to my heart so I'll know when I shouldn't get involved in conversations that aren't pleasing to You. I'm so glad to belong to You. Help me not to do anything to make You ashamed of me.

A Virtuous Woman in Today's World

*"Who can find a virtuous woman? for her price is far above rubies.
The heart of her husband doth safely trust in her, so that he shall
have no need of spoil. She will do him good and not evil all the
days of her life. She seeketh wool, and flax, and worketh willingly
with her hands. She is like the merchants' ships; she bringeth her
food from afar. . . . She looketh well to the ways of her household,
and eateth not the bread of idleness. . . . Favour is deceitful,
and beauty is vain: but a woman that feareth
the LORD, she shall be praised."*

PROVERBS 31:10–14, 27, 30 KJV

In today's world, women are encouraged to dress sexy and flaunt
their bodies. Virtue seems to have lost its value. How can we keep
from being influenced by the media in our lifestyle?

....

....

....

....

As Christians, we must value our virtue above being acceptable to
the world. We must keep our lives clean so that others can see a
difference in us. Pray about your influence with others.

....

....

....

....

If you're married, you want your husband to trust you. What are some ways you can help him to safely trust in you? If you're looking for ways to be a blessing to your husband, pray for God's direction in your marriage. Ask Him to make you a blessing to your husband.

....

....

....

Many women work outside the home. In what ways can women today be good wives and mothers even when their responsibilities extend beyond the home?

....

....

....

Spend time praying for your husband, family, and home. Ask God to give you direction in being a virtuous woman.

....

....

....

Jesus, help me not to be influenced by the world. Help me to use wisdom in the way I dress and conduct myself. Help me to remember that modesty and virtue are important to You. Show me how to be a godly woman who doesn't embarrass You or my husband or family by the way I act. Help me to be a blessing to my husband and not a hindrance. I want him to trust me in every area of our lives together. Help me not to do anything that will bring You or him shame or pain. Give me the strength to be the kind of woman You want me to be and the wife and mother my family needs.

A Clean Heart

Purge me with hyssop, and I shall be clean: wash me, and I shall be whiter than snow. Make me to hear joy and gladness; that the bones which thou hast broken may rejoice. Hide thy face from my sins, and blot out all mine iniquities. Create in me a clean heart, O God; and renew a right spirit within me. Cast me not away from thy presence; and take not thy holy spirit from me. Restore unto me the joy of thy salvation; and uphold me with thy free spirit.

PSALM 51:7–12 KJV

The twigs of the hyssop bush were used for sprinkling in ancient Jewish rites of purification. The psalmist was concerned with being pure and clean before God. As Christians, we should have this same desire. If you're feeling this same need, talk to God about it.

....

....

....

....

Sometimes the stress of life can cause us to lose our joy, but we can also lose it if we have done something to displease the Lord. Ask God to search your heart for anything that might keep you from experiencing the joy He wants to give.

....

....

....

....

....

We cannot clean up our own heart or renew a right spirit within ourselves. God does it for us. Ask Him to give you a clean heart and to renew a right spirit within you.

....

....

....

Living outside the presence of God opens us up to evil influences. Seek God for a deeper relationship with Him as you pray.

....

....

....

If you have lost the joy of salvation, are there things you need to do to have that joy restored?

....

....

....

Lord, just like the writer who wrote this prayer, I need You to wash me and make me clean again. I can't do it within myself. Forgive me for the things I've done that keep me from being clean before You. Only You can cleanse me and make me pure. I want to experience Your joy again. Take away those things that steal my joy. Search my heart and show me if there is something keeping me from hearing Your voice, from feeling joyful. Make me glad again. Forgive me of any sin that has come between You and me. Create a clean heart within me and give me the right spirit. I want to experience Your presence in my life and feel Your Holy Spirit guiding me.

Watch Yourself, Not Others

Brothers and sisters, if someone is caught in a sin, you who live by the Spirit should restore that person gently. But watch yourselves, or you also may be tempted. Carry each other's burdens, and in this way you will fulfill the law of Christ. If anyone thinks they are something when they are not, they deceive themselves. Each one should test their own actions. Then they can take pride in themselves alone, without comparing themselves to someone else, for each one should carry their own load. . . . Do not be deceived: God cannot be mocked. A man reaps what he sows.

GALATIANS 6:1–5, 7 NIV

It's easy to judge someone for his or her sin if we're not careful. This scripture tells us to restore that person gently. If you know of someone who has been involved in the wrong thing, pray for him or her. What are some ways you can be a blessing to that person?

....

....

....

We must be on our guard at all times, because none of us are above temptation. How can we avoid giving in to temptation?

....

....

....

Pray for those around you who may be dealing with temptation. In this way, you can help carry their burden.

....

....

What are some ways people deceive themselves? How can we test our own actions and know if they are pleasing to God?

....

....

....

....

....

Each person is responsible for his or her own life. We can't compare ourselves to others and decide if we're pleasing to God or if they're falling short. As you pray, ask God to direct your mind and help you carry your own load.

....

....

....

....

....

Lord, I've been guilty of judging others and how they live. Forgive me. I'm not in their shoes. I don't know what they're going through. Help me to love them and pray for them. Set a guard over my mouth so that I won't talk about them or criticize them. Take my eyes off people and help me look at You. Except for Your grace, I could be in their shoes. Help me to avoid giving in to temptation when it comes my way. Make me strong and bold to stand against that temptation through the help of the Holy Spirit. Take away any prideful thoughts, and help me to carry my own load.

Encourage Yourself

And it came to pass, when David and his men were come to Ziklag on the third day, that the Amalekites had invaded the south, and Ziklag, and smitten Ziklag, and burned it with fire; and had taken the women captives, that were therein: they slew not any, either great or small, but carried them away, and went on their way. So David and his men came to the city, and, behold, it was burned with fire; and their wives, and their sons, and their daughters, were taken captives. Then David and the people that were with him lifted up their voice and wept, until they had no more power to weep. . . . And David was greatly distressed; for the people spake of stoning him, because the soul of all the people was grieved, every man for his sons and for his daughters: but David encouraged himself in the Lord his God.

1 Samuel 30:1–4, 6 KJV

David and his men faced a terrible tragedy. Their city was burned and their families carried away. If you're facing hard times in your life, put your faith and confidence in God. As you pray, ask for strength to walk through these times.

....

....

....

If you've cried until you have no strength left to cry, pour out your heart to God. He not only hears us when we pray but also is aware of our deepest pain and understands our tears.

....

....

....

When David reached the end of his rope, he encouraged himself in the Lord. What are you doing to encourage yourself in the Lord?

....

....

....

....

How can you help other members of your family understand God's power to help them?

....

....

....

....

What are some ways you can help others who are dealing with tragedy in their lives?

....

....

....

....

Lord, I don't know how to deal with what I'm facing. It's more than I can stand. How can I make it through this? The pain is overwhelming, and I can't stop crying. I need Your help. Give me the faith I need to endure this problem. Help me to have confidence in Your ability to see me through. It seems like everyone is against me and nobody understands what I'm facing. But I know You care and understand. Show me how to be encouraged in You, and help me to be a blessing to others who are facing hard times.

Whom Do You Belong To?

And they found an Egyptian in the field, and brought him to David, and gave him bread, and he did eat; and they made him drink water; and they gave him a piece of a cake of figs, and two clusters of raisins: and when he had eaten, his spirit came again to him: for he had eaten no bread, nor drunk any water, three days and three nights. And David said unto him, To whom belongest thou? and whence art thou? And he said, I am a young man of Egypt, servant to an Amalekite; and my master left me, because three days agone I fell sick.

1 SAMUEL 30:11–13 KJV

If you're facing trouble and it looks as though there's no way out, remind yourself to whom you belong. You're a daughter of God, and His power is limitless.

....

....

....

....

What are some benefits of belonging to God? Take time to list all your blessings and realize they came from Him; then spend time in prayer thanking Him for those blessings.

....

....

....

....

....

If you are taking on new responsibilities and it's causing you anxiety or maybe fear, this is another good time to ask yourself, *To whom do I belong?* It's Satan's business to magnify your fears and temporarily blind you to God's power.

Revisit times in your past when God delivered you from trouble or carried you through bad times. He doesn't change. He can do it again. Ask Him.

Praise God in the bad times as well as the good. Remember, you belong to Him and He welcomes your praises. Spend some time telling Him how much you love and appreciate His goodness.

Lord, You know what I'm facing. I can't fix it. It looks like there's no way out, that it's impossible. But I'm Your child; I belong to You. You've never failed me before. You've always been there for me. Thank You for all those other times You've brought me through. As I go through this valley, hold my hand, just like a father who holds the hand of his little child. Don't allow Satan to blind me to Your love and concern for me. I'm so glad I belong to You. I give You praise today for Your presence in my life. I know You'll see me through. Thank You for Your blessings on my life.

Jesus Understands Your Pain

And he was teaching in one of the synagogues on the sabbath. And, behold, there was a woman which had a spirit of infirmity eighteen years, and was bowed together, and could in no wise lift up herself. And when Jesus saw her, he called her to him, and said unto her, Woman, thou art loosed from thine infirmity. And he laid his hands on her: and immediately she was made straight, and glorified God.

LUKE 13:10–13 KJV

What physical problems are you, or a family member, facing today?

....

....

....

Sometimes our problems are magnified by our fear of what could happen. When fear takes over, our thinking isn't always rational. Talk to God about your problem; ask Him to give you peace in place of your fear.

....

....

....

Jesus came that we could have salvation, but He also suffered in His body for our benefit. He was beaten and suffered cruel treatment at the hands of those who hated Him. He understands your pain. He knows what it is to hurt. Talk with Him about the pain you feel.

....

....

....

....

Jesus healed the woman in the synagogue who had been suffering
for eighteen years. The physical issue she suffered and the length
of time she'd had it didn't have any effect on the power of Jesus to
heal her. Don't allow your situation to keep you from believing by
faith that He can do the same for you.

....

....

....

When you pray, ask Jesus to give you strength for what lies ahead.
Anything is possible with God. Trust that He knows best and will
see you through your illness.

....

....

....

*Jesus, I'm scared. You know I'm sick and what I've been told can
happen. Sometimes my mind goes wild and I imagine terrible things.
Please take away this irrational fear I feel and give me Your peace
in place of it. I know You have experienced pain. You know what I'm
going through. But sometimes, the pain is more than I can stand.
Please help me be able to deal with the pain. Strengthen me. You
know my diagnosis, and You know what lies ahead for me. I know
You are able to heal me. This illness is not too much for Your healing
power. I know all things are possible with God. Help me to trust You
no matter what may happen.*

Ask for Wisdom

Consider it pure joy, my brothers and sisters, whenever you face trials of many kinds, because you know that the testing of your faith produces perseverance. Let perseverance finish its work so that you may be mature and complete, not lacking anything. If any of you lacks wisdom, you should ask God, who gives generously to all without finding fault, and it will be given to you. But when you ask, you must believe and not doubt, because the one who doubts is like a wave of the sea, blown and tossed by the wind. That person should not expect to receive anything from the Lord.

JAMES 1:2–7 NIV

How is it possible to be joyful when you're going through a trial?

....

....

....

....

If we face the test and pass, we know it produces perseverance, but sometimes it's hard to stand the test. What are some things you can do to make it through the testing?

....

....

....

....

We all want to be mature Christians, but our human nature sometimes gets in the way. What keeps you from being all you need to be for Christ? Pray about those things that hinder you.

....

....

....

If you feel you need more wisdom, talk to God about it. He will not criticize you for needing more wisdom but will give it freely.

....

....

....

God wants us to believe Him completely for those things we need. A lack of faith may keep us from receiving what we ask Him for. If you haven't received the answers you're looking for, pray that God will increase your faith to trust Him.

....

....

....

Lord, it's hard to be happy or feel joyful right now. I'm having a hard time with this problem. I know if I pass the test, it will make me stronger as a Christian, but that doesn't make it any easier. Help me to stand the test of my faith. You know the things that keep me from being as mature as I need to be. Help me to resist the temptation to give in. You know I need more wisdom to deal with this situation. Give me the wisdom I need to handle the problems I come in contact with. I know You want me to have more wisdom, so I accept Your gift given so freely. Increase my faith so that I may believe You for whatever I need.

Seek Peace, Pursue It

Finally, all of you, be like-minded, be sympathetic, love one another, be compassionate and humble. Do not repay evil with evil or insult with insult. On the contrary, repay evil with blessing, because to this you were called so that you may inherit a blessing. For, "Whoever would love life and see good days must keep their tongue from evil and their lips from deceitful speech. They must turn from evil and do good; they must seek peace and pursue it. For the eyes of the Lord are on the righteous and his ears are attentive to their prayer, but the face of the Lord is against those who do evil."

1 Peter 3:8–12 NIV

If someone has hurt you and you're finding it hard to be compassionate and sympathetic to that person because he or she mistreated you, what thoughts are going through your mind?

....

....

....

....

When someone insults you, what is your first reaction? If you're inclined to repay that person with an insult of your own, ask God to help you speak words of peace.

....

....

....

....

If we want to inherit a blessing from God, He wants us to repay evil with blessing. How do we do this?

....

....

....

Words spoken can never be taken back. We may be forgiven, but what we have said may never be forgotten. Ask God to give you soft answers in times of anger.

....

....

....

When you pray, pray that your speech will be acceptable before God and man. Ask God to make you a peacemaker and to help you seek peace with those you come in contact with.

....

....

....

Lord, I'm so angry and hurt because of the way I've been treated. I don't understand why that person said those things to me. Even worse is the shame I feel for what I said in return. Forgive me for those harsh words I spoke. Your Word tells us to pursue peace, but sometimes I have a hard time doing that with certain people. Help me to watch what I say. Give me the right words to speak even to those who hurt me. Don't let me have a desire for revenge. Help me love them and not repay evil with evil. Let my speech be acceptable to You and those around me. Give me soft answers for those who insult me. Make me a peacemaker.

God Is My Defense

*Truly my soul waiteth upon God: from him cometh my salvation.
He only is my rock and my salvation; he is my defence; I shall
not be greatly moved. . . . My soul, wait thou only upon God;
for my expectation is from him. . . . In God is my salvation
and my glory: the rock of my strength, and my refuge,
is in God. Trust in him at all times; ye people, pour out
your heart before him: God is a refuge for us.*

PSALM 62:1–2, 5, 7–8 KJV

We live in a fast-paced world. It's easy to get caught up in the whirl-wind of technology and what the world feeds us. Instead of waiting on God, we want instant gratification. Who or what are you waiting on today? Is your confidence in God or man?

....

....

....

....

Whenever we face tough times, life can get shaky. People have a tendency to rely on what the world offers, but God is our Rock. What are some ways we can lean on Him so we won't be moved by the turbulence around us?

....

....

....

....

How would you classify your relationship with God? If it's not as solid as you'd like it to be, time spent in prayer will reinforce it.

....

....

....

Is your time with God a matter of routine? How long has it been since you poured out your heart to Him and trusted Him with your deepest feelings? He wants you to share with Him.

....

....

....

God is a refuge for us, a safe place to go when it seems everyone else has abandoned us. The key to finding and living in this refuge is waiting upon Him and trusting Him completely. Do you find it hard to wait and trust Him?

....

....

....

Lord, thank You for being my Rock, my Salvation, and my Defense. When I can't fight my battles, I know You'll be there for me. Help me wait upon You and not get in a hurry to fix things myself. Help me rely on You and not what the world has to offer. I want a stronger relationship with You. Help me to draw closer to You. Help me to set aside those things that keep me from spending more time with You. I don't want our relationship to be just a daily routine. I want it to be an intimate relationship. Help me to trust You with everything, big or little.

Walk upon High Places

Though the fig tree does not bud and there are no grapes on the vines, though the olive crop fails and the fields produce no food, though there are no sheep in the pen and no cattle in the stalls, yet I will rejoice in the Lord, I will be joyful in God my Savior. The Sovereign Lord is my strength; he makes my feet like the feet of a deer, he enables me to tread on the heights.

HABAKKUK 3:17–19 NIV

What situations are you facing today in your finances, job, or family?

....

....

....

It's easy to grumble when things aren't as we would like them. We're all faced with uncomfortable circumstances from time to time. When you're faced with loss, how do you handle it?

....

....

....

The writer of this passage lists several problems: food is short, the crops have failed, and he no longer has his livestock. But instead of grumbling, he has chosen to rejoice in the Lord. Have you rejoiced in your present situation, or has grumbling taken over?

....

....

....

What are you focusing on? Your problems or God? When we take our focus off God, it's natural to become discouraged because we've lost our source of hope. Talking to Him about your problems can put your focus back where it belongs.

....

....

....

....

God is our Strength. He makes us walk in high places even when things look hopeless. Spend some time in prayer, thanking God for what you do have, surrendering the problem to Him, and stepping out by faith onto the high places in Him.

....

....

....

....

....

Lord, You know the things I've lost and what I'm in need of. The situation looks hopeless, but I know You're in charge if I let You be. In the past, I've sometimes tied Your hands by trying to take care of everything myself. We both know that didn't turn out too good. I'm sorry for complaining and feeling resentful about this situation. Help me not to grumble and complain. You've blessed me and provided for me in the past. I know You will continue to do so. Thank You for the way You've taken care of me. Help me to praise You even in the time of loss. Turn my focus on You instead of the problem. Enable me to walk in Your high places.

The Son Is Life

*He that hath the Son hath life; and he that hath not the Son
of God hath not life. These things have I written unto you that
believe on the name of the Son of God; that ye may know that ye
have eternal life, and that ye may believe on the name of the Son
of God. And this is the confidence that we have in him, that,
if we ask any thing according to his will, he heareth us: and if
we know that he hear us, whatsoever we ask, we know
that we have the petitions that we desired of him.*

1 John 5:12–15 KJV

If you have the Son, you have life. What does this mean to you? If
you remember what life was like before you accepted Christ, you
know how different it is now.

....

....

....

Are you facing something that makes you feel vulnerable? When
we place our confidence in God, instead of ourselves, our thinking
can change.

....

....

....

If we have confidence in God, we can ask anything according to His
will and He hears us. How do we know if something is according
to God's will?

....

....

....

....

....

Sometimes our will and God's will collide because we want our own way. We have already decided what we're going to do. And when God speaks to us, letting us know He has other plans, it's hard to submit to His will. If you find yourself in this place, spend time praying about surrendering your will to Him.

....

....

....

....

How can we have the faith to believe that we have the petitions that we desire of God? Take time to remember those petitions from the past and how God answered them.

....

....

....

....

Lord, thank You for the life You've given me. Without You, I wouldn't really be living. I would only exist. Your Word tells me I can ask anything according to Your will and You will hear my request. How do I always know when it's Your will? How can I be sure? Give me the confidence in You that I need so there will be no question in my mind about whether You hear me. Increase my faith in You and Your Word. Let my requests be pleasing to You, and let the desires of my heart be centered on You and Your will.

Planting Good Seed

Then he told them many things in parables, saying: "A farmer went out to sow his seed. As he was scattering the seed, some fell along the path, and the birds came and ate it up. Some fell on rocky places, where it did not have much soil. It sprang up quickly, because the soil was shallow. But when the sun came up, the plants were scorched, and they withered because they had no root. Other seed fell among thorns, which grew up and choked the plants. Still other seed fell on good soil, where it produced a crop—a hundred, sixty or thirty times what was sown."

MATTHEW 13:3–8 NIV

What kind of seed are you sowing into your life and the lives of others?

....

....

....

Some of the seed planted by the farmer came up; but the birds ate it. Some of it was scorched by the sun. Still other seeds were choked out by thorns. He appears to be a careless planter, but he didn't have control over everything. What kind of planter are you, and what kind of seeds are you planting?

....

....

....

Sometimes we feel all our work is for nothing; however, it may not be the work we're doing, but where we planted that work. Where are you concentrating your efforts?

....

....

....

....

If you would like to see your efforts accomplish more, pray that God will direct you to the people and places where you can plant for Him.

....

....

....

....

How should you view your Christian walk in light of the scripture passage today?

....

....

....

....

Lord, sometimes I work so hard and it doesn't feel like I'm getting anywhere. I try to be a good witness for You. I want to see others find You and become a part of the kingdom, but I haven't seen that many people saved. I invite people to church, but they don't come. I work hard to plant seeds in other people's lives, but I don't always see results. All my efforts seem to be a waste of time. Please show me what I need to do to win others to You. Show me what efforts are pleasing to You. Help me not to worry about whether I'm noticed or get any credit, but help my seed to fall on good soil and produce a good crop for Your kingdom.

The Spirit Gives Life

Those who live according to the flesh have their minds set on what the flesh desires; but those who live in accordance with the Spirit have their minds set on what the Spirit desires. The mind governed by the flesh is death, but the mind governed by the Spirit is life and peace. . . . Those who are in the realm of the flesh cannot please God. . . . But if Christ is in you, then even though your body is subject to death because of sin, the Spirit gives life because of righteousness. . . . For those who are led by the Spirit of God are the children of God.

ROMANS 8:5–6, 8, 10, 14 NIV

As a woman, what is your mind set on today?

....

....

....

Sometimes other people can influence our thoughts as well as what we read, view online, or see on television. Who or what is influencing your thoughts?

....

....

....

If we live according to the flesh, then our minds will be set on doing what pleases us. Those who live according to God's Spirit want to please Him. Sometimes we get caught up in trying to please other people. Who are you trying to please?

....

....

....

....

Living to please ourselves or others interferes with our relationship with God. Spending time with Him in prayer brings our thoughts back into proper focus. Ask God to help you focus on Him first.

....

....

....

....

We have choices to make every day. We can choose flesh or Spirit, death or life. It's up to us. As you pray, ask God to help you make the choice to be led by His Spirit. Those who are led by the Spirit experience life in Christ.

....

....

....

....

Lord, there are so many voices calling to me, some good, some bad, all trying to influence me on how to live my life. Sometimes I want to follow voices that I know aren't good for me, but they look and sound good. And it seems everyone else is following them. It's easy to get caught up in what everyone else is doing. Help me to make choices that please You. Give me strength to resist temptations that are wrong. I need to rely on You to direct my decisions and my choices. I want to be led by Your Spirit and experience life with You. Don't let me be influenced by other people's decisions.

To Obey Is Best

Samuel said, "Although you were once small in your own eyes, did you not become the head of the tribes of Israel? The Lord anointed you king over Israel. And he sent you on a mission, saying, 'Go and completely destroy those wicked people, the Amalekites; wage war against them until you have wiped them out.' Why did you not obey the Lord? Why did you pounce on the plunder and do evil in the eyes of the Lord?" . . . "Does the Lord delight in burnt offerings and sacrifices as much as in obeying the Lord? To obey is better than sacrifice, and to heed is better than the fat of rams."

1 Samuel 15:17–19, 22 niv

What kind of mission or task has the Lord spoken to you about? What are your feelings about what He has asked you to do?

....

....

....

....

How do you view yourself? If you feel unqualified, as Saul did when he was anointed king over Israel, pray about your qualifications. God has a reason for choosing you. He doesn't see you as you see yourself.

....

....

....

....

If you feel you have been disobedient in your task, what do you need to do to set things right in God's eyes?

....

....

....

Sometimes people feel they can avoid what God wants them to do by performing all kinds of "good deeds." How do you think God views this?

....

....

....

Nothing can take the place of obedience. Pray about any situation in your life where you feel you haven't obeyed God's voice.

....

....

....

Lord, I know what You want me to do, but I'm not qualified to do that job. I don't have the education or training I need. Who am I to step into that position and carry out that work? Other people will know I'm not qualified either, and You know what they will say: "Who does she think she is?" I want to do the right thing, but there are other things I'd rather do. Forgive me for having that attitude. I know if You ask me to do something, I should be obedient no matter what. Please help me to forget about what others think and concentrate on answering Your call. Help me not to try to substitute something else in place of Your will. Help me to remember that it's better to obey than sacrifice.

Replacing What Has Been Lost

The company of the prophets said to Elisha, "Look, the place where we meet with you is too small for us. Let us go to the Jordan, where each of us can get a pole; and let us build a place there for us to meet."... They went to the Jordan and began to cut down trees. As one of them was cutting down a tree, the iron axhead fell into the water. "Oh no, my lord!" he cried out. "It was borrowed!" The man of God asked, "Where did it fall?" When he showed him the place, Elisha cut a stick and threw it there, and made the iron float. "Lift it out," he said. Then the man reached out his hand and took it.

2 Kings 6:1–2, 4–7 NIV

Even while working for God, sometimes we lose things we need. It might be something essential to our work, just as the man lost the ax head while cutting a tree. The man in the scripture passage immediately called on Elisha, his master, for help. When you feel loss, what is your first response?

....

....

....

....

What are some things you've lost in your Christian walk?

....

....

....

....

It's easy sometimes to blame others or grumble about a situation. When we call on God, He is beside us ready to help in whatever circumstance we find ourselves, but it's up to us to call on Him. Why do we sometimes forget to call on God instead of relying on ourselves?

....

....

....

....

....

In your prayer time, ask God to restore those things you have lost in your spiritual walk.

....

....

....

....

....

God, my walk with You isn't what it should be. I've lost some things along the way. I was so busy working and doing what I thought I should do for You that I let some things slip. Forgive me for allowing that to happen. Help me not to substitute work or good deeds for my relationship with You. I know You can restore those things I've lost and get me back on track. It will take a miracle, but I know You can do it. Just like the ax head that came to the surface, I know You can do the same for me. Help me to reach out and take those losses that You restore to me, and help me to hold on to them tightly in the future.

Hide God's Word in Your Heart

How can a young person stay on the path of purity? By living according to your word. I seek you with all my heart; do not let me stray from your commands. I have hidden your word in my heart that I might not sin against you. Praise be to you, LORD; teach me your decrees. With my lips I recount all the laws that come from your mouth. I rejoice in following your statutes as one rejoices in great riches. I meditate on your precepts and consider your ways. I delight in your decrees; I will not neglect your word.

PSALM 119:9–16 NIV

Sometimes outside influences affect us more than we realize. In light of today's culture, what influences dictate your lifestyle? As you pray, ask God to reveal those influences to you and to show you how to deal with them.

....

....

....

....

The psalmist said he seeks the Lord with all his heart. He was committed to living according to God's Word. Who or what are you committed to with all your heart?

....

....

....

....

....

If you find it hard to resist the pull or influence of the world, pray about your personal commitment to God. Ask the Lord to teach you His decrees.

....

....

....

How much time do you spend reading the Bible? What do you need to do so that God's Word will be hidden in your heart? Before you begin reading, ask the Lord to open your understanding as you read.

....

....

....

When God's Word is hidden in our hearts, we will be able to rejoice in following His precepts and meditate on His ways. What are you meditating on today?

....

....

....

Lord, You know what influences me in my daily life. Are there things that keep me from walking close to You? Am I being influenced in some way that I don't even realize? Open my eyes so that I can see what I need to improve on. Give me a desire to read more of Your Word. Help me to hide Your Word in my heart so I can live in a way that pleases You. Help me not to neglect reading Your Word. I want to make a new commitment to You and Your statutes. As I go through the day, let me meditate on Your Word and consider Your goodness in my life.

What Does God Require?

With what shall I come before the LORD and bow down before the exalted God? Shall I come before him with burnt offerings, with calves a year old? Will the LORD be pleased with thousands of rams, with ten thousand rivers of olive oil? Shall I offer my firstborn for my transgression, the fruit of my body for the sin of my soul? He has shown you, O mortal, what is good. And what does the LORD require of you? To act justly and to love mercy and to walk humbly with your God.

MICAH 6:6–8 NIV

In Old Testament times, people offered animal sacrifices for their sin. Jesus came as the sacrifice for our sin. What does He want from us?

....

....

....

....

What are you willing to offer as a sacrifice to God? What do you think is acceptable?

....

....

....

....

Several questions are asked in these verses. Read the answer again. What does it mean to you as a Christian? If we love mercy, how will that manifest itself in our lives? In what ways do you act justly in your daily life? Other people may not know you are acting in a just manner, but God sees and knows your heart.

....

....

....

....

....

Being humble requires a sacrifice in itself. We must give up our selfish pride and surrender our lives to God before we can walk humbly with Him. What will this require of you? Ask God to help you be more humble before Him.

....

....

....

....

....

Jesus, thank You for coming as the ultimate sacrifice for my sin. Even though I was unworthy, You died for me. I want to do what You require of me. I want to walk humbly before You, but I realize I need to get rid of my own selfish will and pride. I need to sacrifice those things that keep me from walking in a way that pleases You. Help me to do the right thing even when no one is watching. Show me how to love mercy and extend that mercy to others. Give me the courage to surrender my own will to You so that I can walk humbly before You.

Are You Thirsty?

"Come, all you who are thirsty, come to the waters; and you who have no money, come, buy and eat! Come, buy wine and milk without money and without cost. Why spend money on what is not bread, and your labor on what does not satisfy? Listen, listen to me, and eat what is good, and you will delight in the richest of fare. Give ear and come to me; listen, that you may live.". . . Seek the L<small>ORD</small> while he may be found; call on him while he is near. Let the wicked forsake their ways and the unrighteous their thoughts. Let them turn to the L<small>ORD</small>, and he will have mercy on them, and to our God, for he will freely pardon.

I<small>SAIAH</small> 55:1–3, 6–7 <small>NIV</small>

What does it mean to you to be spiritually thirsty or hungry? How is this different from natural thirst and hunger?

....

....

....

If you're thirsty, what are some ways you can satisfy your spiritual thirst? If we're not careful, we can become spiritually dehydrated.

....

....

....

Sometimes we try to satisfy spiritual hunger and thirst with natural means. Why doesn't this work?

....

....

....

....

....

God offers us what we need without cost. If we accept His offer, it will mean life for us. If there is something lacking in your spiritual walk, talk to God about it in prayer. He offers mercy and pardon to those who come to Him. He will supply what you need.

....

....

....

....

Seeking the Lord on a daily basis can help us stay nourished spiritually. In what ways do you seek Him every day?

....

....

....

....

God, sometimes I feel like I'm starving spiritually. I need more spiritual food than I'm getting. The fault lies with me. I've tried satisfying that need with earthly pleasures and natural food, but it doesn't work. I need more of the food and living water that You provide. Why do I keep trying to satisfy these needs by myself? Help me to seek You every day for what I need in my spiritual life. As I spend more time with You, I know I'll become more satisfied, so why do I waste time on my own efforts? Help me to quit starving myself spiritually. Help me to seek You more often. Thank You for the mercy and pardon that You offer to those who turn to You.

The Good Samaritan

In reply Jesus said: "A man was going down from Jerusalem to Jericho, when he was attacked by robbers. They stripped him of his clothes, beat him and went away, leaving him half dead. A priest happened to be going down the same road, and when he saw the man, he passed by on the other side. So too, a Levite, when he came to the place and saw him, passed by on the other side. But a Samaritan, as he traveled, came where the man was; and when he saw him, he took pity on him. He went to him and bandaged his wounds, pouring on oil and wine. Then he put the man on his own donkey brought him to an inn and took care of him."

LUKE 10:30–34 NIV

As a woman, living in our violent society, how do you feel about helping a stranger?

....

....

....

What do you think God would have you do if you saw someone who needed help?

....

....

....

How are we to view individuals we come in contact with? What should we take into consideration when we make a decision to help someone?

....

....

....

....

The Good Samaritan put aside the fact that Samaritans weren't accepted by Jews. He gave him first aid and then set him on his own donkey, which meant he had to walk. Then he took him to an inn and continued to care for him. How far are you willing to go to help someone in need?

....

....

....

....

Fear may play a part in our stopping to help someone. How do we deal with that fear in light of what God would have us do?

....

....

....

....

Lord, help me to show compassion to those I come in contact with who are in trouble and need my help, but also give me wisdom to know what to do. Don't let me look at the color of their skin, how much money they have, or what their status in life may be. Help me to look past those things and see a human being in need. Help me to set aside prejudice, selfishness, and pride. Give me a heart full of concern and love for my fellow man. Show me how I can be more like You. Make me a Good Samaritan. Help me not to be afraid when You speak to my heart about someone in need.

Living Stones

Therefore, rid yourselves of all malice and all deceit, hypocrisy, envy, and slander of every kind. Like newborn babies, crave pure spiritual milk, so that by it you may grow up in your salvation, now that you have tasted that the Lord is good. As you come to him, the living Stone—rejected by humans but chosen by God and precious to him—you also, like living stones, are being built into a spiritual house to be a holy priesthood, offering spiritual sacrifices acceptable to God through Jesus Christ. . . . Now to you who believe, this stone is precious. But to those who do not believe, "The stone the builders rejected has become the cornerstone."

1 PETER 2:1–5, 7 NIV

What are some things you might want to get rid of in your life? In prayer, ask God to free you from those things.

....

....

....

....

Christians need spiritual milk to develop and grow in their walk with the Lord. What is this spiritual milk and how can we obtain it for ourselves?

....

....

....

....

....

Jesus is the living Stone we should pattern our lives after so we become living stones in a spiritual house. What is a living stone? What could cause a stone to become alive?

....

....

....

....

....

Jesus was rejected by His own people, but He was chosen by God. We also have been chosen to become a part of a holy priesthood. If we are priests of God, how should our lives be different?

What kind of spiritual sacrifices do you need to make to God today?

....

....

....

....

....

Lord, there are things I need to get rid of in my life. Forgive me for allowing them to take root in my heart. Free me from those things, and give me a desire for spiritual milk so that I can grow in You and become the living stone I need to be. I want to be a part of the spiritual house You're building. If I am to be a priest for You, I need help. Show me how to live a priestly life before others. Direct my steps in the way I should walk, and help me to offer spiritual sacrifices that are acceptable to You. Sometimes it's hard to offer a sacrifice because it requires me to set aside my own desires. Help me be willing to do that for You.

Thou Hast Made Me Glad

It is a good thing to give thanks unto the Lord, and to sing praises unto thy name, O Most High: to shew forth thy lovingkindness in the morning, and thy faithfulness every night, upon an instrument of ten strings, and upon the psaltery; upon the harp with a solemn sound. For thou, Lord, hast made me glad through thy work: I will triumph in the works of thy hands. O Lord, how great are thy works! and thy thoughts are very deep. . . . But thou, Lord, art most high for evermore.
PSALM 92:1–5, 8 KJV

Some feel that church is the only place to worship the Lord, but God isn't confined to a building or temple. What other places do you worship the Lord? How often do you praise Him and give Him thanks? In prayer today, spend some time in worship, thanking God for His loving-kindness and His faithfulness.

....

....

....

....

God is always worthy of our gratitude and our praise. What specific things can you be thankful for today?

....

....

....

....

What ways or methods do you use to worship the Lord? God blesses us with different talents and abilities. We can choose to use them for Him or for our own benefit. What ability has He given you, and how do you use it for His glory?

....

....

....

How can we triumph in the works of God's hands? He works in more ways than just our lives. Spend some time thinking about how He takes care of all creation and then praise Him for His greatness.

....

....

....

In what specific ways does the Lord make you glad?

....

....

....

Lord, thank You for giving me a voice to worship You with. Help me to always use it to thank You for Your goodness to me. I praise You for life and the breath I breathe every day. Thank You for being so faithful to me. I've failed You many times, but You've never failed me. I give You praise for that faithfulness in my life. Thank You for blessing me to work for You, worship You, and bring You glory. I'm so glad to know that You're in control of this world and that Your great mercy is extended to all who will receive it. Thou art worthy to receive praise and honor and glory. I worship You today and lift up Your name.

Be Not Afraid

Then the word of the LORD came unto me, saying, Before I formed thee in the belly I knew thee; and before thou camest forth out of the womb I sanctified thee, and I ordained thee a prophet unto the nations. Then said I, Ah, Lord GOD! behold, I cannot speak: for I am a child. But the LORD said unto me, Say not, I am a child: for thou shalt go to all that I shall send thee, and whatsoever I command thee thou shalt speak. Be not afraid of their faces: for I am with thee to deliver thee, saith the LORD. Then the LORD put forth his hand, and touched my mouth. And the LORD said unto me, Behold, I have put my words in thy mouth.

JEREMIAH 1:4–9 KJV

God has something for all of us to do. What specific thing has the Lord called you to do?

....

....

....

Jeremiah's first response was that he couldn't speak. What arguments have you given the Lord for not answering His call?

....

....

....

The Lord told Jeremiah not to be afraid of their faces. If you're afraid to speak to others or in public places, what part does fear play in your decision not to obey God? In prayer, ask God to give you peace in place of the fear.

....

....

The Lord has promised to be with us when we stand before people. Ask Him to increase your faith in Him and His promises so you can do what He has asked of you.

When God calls you, He equips you. He put His words in Jeremiah's mouth so he would know what to speak. Ask God to equip you for the work He has called you to.

Lord, I'm really afraid to do what You're asking me to do. What will people think? I don't have the training that others have. There are plenty of other people who could do what You asked. I want to obey You and please You, but I'm scared, intimidated, and I guess a little proud. Please give me courage to do this. I can't do it alone. Forgive me. In place of my fear, give me Your peace. Help me not to be intimidated by what others think and say, and help me put my trust in You to believe that You will equip me for this job.

Dealing with Giants

And there went out a champion out of the camp of the Philistines, named Goliath, of Gath, whose height was six cubits and a span. . . . And the Philistine said, I defy the armies of Israel this day; give me a man, that we may fight together. . . . And when the Philistine looked about, and saw David, he disdained him: for he was but a youth, and ruddy, and of a fair countenance. . . . Then said David to the Philistine, Thou comest to me with a sword, and with a spear, and with a shield: but I come to thee in the name of the Lord of hosts, the God of the armies of Israel, whom thou hast defied.

1 Samuel 17:4, 10, 42, 45 KJV

Goliath was an imposing figure who frightened those around him. What giants are you facing in your life? Whatever your giant looks like, he's no match for God.

....

....

....

If you're fighting a giant, he's not just defying you; he's defying the Lord of your life, Jesus Christ. You're not in the battle alone. In prayer, ask God for help to fight your battle.

....

....

....

Satan would like for you to think of yourself as small and helpless. It's a lie. David was just a young, untrained warrior, but he faced his giant in the name of the Lord of hosts, the God of Israel. Ask God to help you see yourself through His eyes.

....

....

....

David used a sling and a stone, but he relied on God for supernatural strength and power. Ask God for the spiritual weapons you need for your battle.

....

....

....

Giants aren't easily defeated if we try to do it on our own. Rely on God to fight for you.

....

....

....

God, I have a giant in my life. You know who and what I'm facing. I need Your help. I'm not strong enough by myself to fight this giant. It's bigger and stronger than I am. Who am I? I'm nothing in the face of this terror. Just as You were with David when he faced Goliath, I need You to be with me. Help me to become a spiritual warrior. Give me the spiritual weapons I need to defeat this enemy. I'm relying on You because in myself I can do nothing. I know that all things are possible with You. Help me fight this giant.

What God Has Cleansed

About noon the following day as they were on their journey and approaching the city, Peter went up on the roof to pray. He became hungry and wanted something to eat, and while the meal was being prepared, he fell into a trance. He saw heaven opened and something like a large sheet being let down to earth by its four corners. It contained all kinds of four-footed animals, as well as reptiles and birds. Then a voice told him, "Get up, Peter. Kill and eat." "Surely not, Lord!" Peter replied. "I have never eaten anything impure or unclean." The voice spoke to him a second time, "Do not call anything impure that God has made clean."

Acts 10:9–15 NIV

God used the natural act of eating to teach Peter, and us, a lesson. What do you think is the lesson for you here?

....

....

....

....

Peter had been taught to eat only those animals considered clean under Jewish law.

....

....

....

....

Sometimes we allow what we've been taught to limit what God can do in our lives. Ask God to show you the ways you are limiting

Him in your life. God isn't controlled or limited by man's law. In light of that fact, what things in your life would you like to see God change?

....

....

....

Sometimes we judge others' lives by what we see on the outside. We need to remember that God looks at the heart. If He has made them clean, then they are clean. Ask God to help you not to judge others.

....

....

....

Jesus can free us from impure things that keep us from being clean. If you examined your own "sheet," what kinds of things would you find that might be unclean? During prayer time, ask Him to remove any impurities in your life and make you clean.

....

....

....

Jesus, regardless of what I've been taught or believe, You alone can see my heart and You know if there are things that shouldn't be there. I need to make some changes in life. You know what they are. Show me the impurities in my life that I need to be free of. Help me not to limit You, but have faith that You can do whatever is necessary to make me clean. Help me not to judge others and point out their faults; help me to realize that whatever You have made clean in their lives is clean before You regardless of what I or anyone else may think.

Nothing Can Separate Us from Christ

Who shall separate us from the love of Christ? shall tribulation, or distress, or persecution, or famine, or nakedness, or peril, or sword? As it is written, For thy sake we are killed all the day long; we are accounted as sheep for the slaughter. Nay, in all these things we are more than conquerors through him that loved us. For I am persuaded, that neither death, nor life, nor angels, nor principalities, nor powers, nor things present, nor things to come, nor height, nor depth, nor any other creature, shall be able to separate us from the love of God, which is in Christ Jesus our Lord.

ROMANS 8:35–39 KJV

Sometimes when we face trouble in our lives, we question why God allows it to happen. What was your relationship with Christ like during a tough time in your life? Did it feel as though He wasn't listening?

....

....

....

....

Despite how we may feel during trials or problems, when it's over, we realize Jesus was there all the time. He never left us. We can trust Him to be with us at all times. What are some things you can do to help you stay focused on Jesus during bad times?

....

....

....

....

If you are facing distress, spiritual warfare, or tragedy in your life, spend time talking to God about the problem. Ask Him to give you the faith to be a conqueror over whatever you're facing.

....
....
....
....
....

If there are members of your family facing the problem with you, share this scripture passage with them and then pray together for direction and comfort.

....
....
....
....
....

Lord, I don't understand what's happening to me or my family. We're in trouble, and we're facing a dark time in our lives. We need Your help. Where are You? Touch our lives and draw us close to You as we go through the days ahead. Let us feel Your love and Your presence in our lives. Your Word says nothing can separate us from You. Help me to stand on that promise and believe it with all my heart. Make me a conqueror over all the things that come against me and my family. Help me to be a blessing to them during this time. Your love is more powerful than any other power on earth, even death. Let Your love shine through me.

No Fancy Words

And I, brethren, when I came to you, came not with excellency of speech or of wisdom, declaring unto you the testimony of God. For I determined not to know any thing among you, save Jesus Christ, and him crucified. And I was with you in weakness, and in fear, and in much trembling. And my speech and my preaching was not with enticing words of man's wisdom, but in demonstration of the Spirit and of power: that your faith should not stand in the wisdom of men, but in the power of God.

1 CORINTHIANS 2:1–5 KJV

Paul was an educated man, but he didn't use fancy words, or what he called "excellency of speech," to preach the Gospel. He didn't want his listeners to see him. He wanted them to see Christ. Why do we feel we should be any different?

....

....

....

....

Sometimes because we're not trained in a certain area, we may feel unsure of ourselves. If you've ever been asked to speak before a group and felt anxious, what are some things you did to calm your anxiety?

....

....

....

....

If you're afraid to let others see your weaknesses, what is the reason? Pray about those weaknesses and ask Christ to help you overcome them.

....

....

....

Pray about how you approach others when you share Christ with them. Like Paul, be determined not to share anything except Christ and Him crucified.

....

....

....

Does your faith stand in the wisdom of what others say or do, or does your faith stand in the power of God?

....

....

....

Lord, I want to share You with others, but You know my faults and my weaknesses. I'm afraid of doing certain things because I feel inadequate in those areas. I don't want people to see my bad side, but I don't want to put on a front either. In my attempts to share You with others, take away the pride that keeps me from being sincere. Help me to overcome those anxieties and fears. I need to rely on You and not my abilities. My words have no power to save or deliver people, but Yours do. Help me to share You with those who need Your help. As I rely on You and not my own wisdom or abilities, may those I come in contact with see You and experience Your love for themselves.

Put On Your Armor

Finally, be strong in the Lord and in his mighty power. Put on the full armor of God, so that you can take your stand against the devil's schemes. For our struggle is not against flesh and blood, but against the rulers, against the authorities, against the powers of this dark world and against the spiritual forces of evil in the heavenly realms. Therefore put on the full armor of God, so that when the day of evil comes, you may be able to stand your ground, and after you have done everything, to stand.
EPHESIANS 6:10–13 NIV

What does it mean to you to put on the full armor of God? What do you need to do to be in full armor? For more about the armor, read verses 14–17.

....

....

....

....

We cannot fight against Satan and his schemes if we're not wearing spiritual armor. Man-made weapons won't work in this warfare. We must rely on the Lord and His mighty power to help us be prepared. Ask God to show you how to fight in this battle.

....

....

....

....

....

Soldiers train for battle. They can't afford to go into battle without proper training or they will be defeated. What should you be doing to train for the spiritual battles to come?

....

....

....

Prayer is one of our greatest weapons. The more time we spend in prayer, the better equipped we will be to face our enemy. As you pray, ask God for a deeper prayer life.

....

....

....

After we've done everything we know to do in preparation, we must stand our ground. How do you go about standing your ground in spiritual warfare?

....

....

....

Lord, I want to be ready to face the enemy when he comes, but I can't do it alone. Help me to be strong through You and Your power. Teach me the importance of putting on the armor of God and taking a stand against the enemy. Give me wisdom to fight the battles that come my way. I can't fight spiritual forces of evil and powers of darkness alone; I must have Your strength and help at all times. Help me not to go out into the world without the armor of God covering me. Train me through Your Word and Your wisdom to stand my ground and not allow Satan to defeat me. Help me to be a true soldier for You, always wearing Your armor.

Are You Overwhelmed?

*Hear my cry, O God; attend unto my prayer. From the end
of the earth will I cry unto thee, when my heart is overwhelmed:
lead me to the rock that is higher than I. For thou hast
been a shelter for me, and a strong tower from the enemy.
I will abide in thy tabernacle for ever: I will trust in the
covert of thy wings. For thou, O God, hast heard
my vows: thou hast given me the heritage
of those that fear thy name.*

PSALM 61:1–5 KJV

What's causing you to feel overwhelmed today? Spend time talking to God about the things that are overwhelming you.

....

....

....

....

On those days when it seems there's more than you can handle, cry out to God for strength. When you feel you can't take any more trouble, you have a shelter in Him.

....

....

....

....

When things are at their worst and we can't seem to feel God's presence in our lives, we sometimes think God isn't listening to us. We must have faith during those times that He's still with us. What can you do to strengthen your faith and reassure yourself of His presence?

....

....

....

When we try to solve problems on our own, we exhibit an independence from God. He wants us to rely on Him. How can we put aside our own attempts at working things out and let God take over in our lives?

....

....

....

As you pray, ask God to take charge of the things that overwhelm you.

....

....

....

God, please help me. I'm feeling overwhelmed by everything that's happening in my life right now. I can't take it anymore. I must have Your help. I feel like I'm drowning in all this trouble. You are my Rock on higher ground, my shelter from this storm I'm going through. Please strengthen me and help me to rely on You. Sometimes I can't feel Your presence in my life, but I trust You're still here with me, and I'm asking for Your help. I can't take care of this problem by myself. I've tried and failed. Give me faith to believe in Your ability to see me through this situation. Take charge of the things that overwhelm me.

The Greatest of These Is Love

If I speak in the tongues of men or of angels, but do not have
love, I am only a resounding gong or a clanging cymbal. . . .
Love is patient, love is kind. It does not envy, it does not boast,
it is not proud. It does not dishonor others, it is not self-seeking,
it is not easily angered, it keeps no record of wrongs. Love does
not delight in evil but rejoices with the truth. It always protects,
always trusts, always hopes, always perseveres.

1 CORINTHIANS 13:1, 4–7 NIV

We can usually tell when others are sincere in their feelings toward us. Likewise, others know when we're sincere toward them. How do we attain the kind of sincere love that makes us mean what we say instead of just making a lot of noise?

....

....

....

....

....

When we love someone, we tend to be more patient and kind with that person. Why don't we treat everyone that way?

....

....

....

....

....

What makes it harder to love some people than others? When you pray, ask God to help you love those who are hard to love.

....

....

....

To be Christlike is to love. He loved us so much that He died for us. How many people are willing to make that kind of sacrifice for others? Are you willing?

....

....

....

In love, there is protection, trust, hope, and peace. In prayer, ask God for the kind of love in your life that provides all that to those around you.

....

....

....

Jesus, You loved me so much that You died for me. You loved me when I wasn't very lovable. Help me to extend that same kind of love to others. You know I have a hard time loving some people. They just rub me the wrong way. I don't like the things they say and do. But, I'm sure You probably don't love a lot of the things I do either. Help me look past the faults of others and love them as You do. I can't do it on my own. I need You to help me love them through You. Give me the kind of love that extends patience and kindness to people regardless of how they treat me. Fill me with the kind of love that protects, trusts, hopes, and perseveres through all kinds of situations.

What Are You Thinking?

*Finally, brethren, whatsoever things are true,
whatsoever things are honest, whatsoever things
are just, whatsoever things are pure, whatsoever things are
lovely, whatsoever things are of good report; if there be
any virtue, and if there be any praise, think on these
things. . . . Let this mind be in you, which
was also in Christ Jesus.*

PHILIPPIANS 4:8; 2:5 KJV

If you're a stay-at-home mom, you're probably focused on your home and family. If you're a working woman, your mind is on your job. But while you're taking care of these responsibilities, what kinds of thoughts slip into your mind?

....

....

....

....

If you have thoughts you're ashamed of, ask God to keep your mind on subjects and ideas that please Him.

....

....

....

....

At one time or another, everyone thinks about something they shouldn't. We can't keep thoughts from flashing through our brains, but we don't have to dwell on them. Sometimes they seem harmless, but if you feel a red flag go up, get rid of those thoughts.

....

....

....

The scripture passage today tells us the kinds of things we need to think about. In prayer, ask God to help you dwell on things that are honest, just, pure, lovely, and of a good report.

....

....

....

What type of material do you feed your mind with? Take a moment and think about the books you read, the television programs you watch, the websites you visit—all these sources influence our thinking. Ask God for guidance in choosing what to feed your mind.

....

....

....

Lord, sometimes I think about things that I know aren't pleasing to You. Sometimes all I have to do is see a person and the wrong kinds of thoughts fill my mind. Please forgive me; help me think of something positive about that person and not concentrate on the negative. Give me the strength to resist those thoughts and not allow them to become a part of me. Help me to make good choices in what I read, watch, or study. Help me not to fill my mind with what the world is focused on, but let the same mind that is in You be in me. Let my mind be filled with thoughts of good, honest, lovely things.

Passing On the Faith

*To Timothy, my dear son: Grace, mercy and peace from God
the Father and Christ Jesus our Lord. . . . I am reminded of your
sincere faith, which first lived in your grandmother Lois and in
your mother Eunice and, I am persuaded, now lives in you also.
For this reason I remind you to fan into flame the gift of
God, which is in you through the laying on of my hands.
For the Spirit God gave us does not make us timid,
but gives us power, love and self-discipline.*

2 Timothy 1:2, 5–7 NIV

Who influenced you to accept Christ and mentored you in the
faith? How did that person do this?

....

....

....

....

As you think about that person's life, what did he or she do that
affected you the most?

....

....

....

....

In what way are you passing on your faith to your children, other
members of your family, or those you come in contact with? During
prayer, ask God to lead you to those who need to be mentored by
you, whether a family member or someone outside the family.

_____

_____

_____

Don't underestimate the power of a life lived for Christ and the impact it can have on those around you. In today's verses, it was Timothy's grandmother and mother who lived out their faith before him. That legacy of faith continued in their family.

_____

_____

_____

What kind of legacy are you going to leave behind after you're gone? Ask God to help you live a life before others that will glorify Him.

_____

_____

_____

Father, thank You for those who encouraged me and led me to accept Jesus as my Savior. I'm so grateful they took the time to tell me about You and to show me how to live out my faith. As I watched their lives, I saw You at work. Now it's my turn to lead someone to You. Give me wisdom and the words I need to show them Your love at work in my life. Help me to live in a way that brings glory to You. Make my faith strong and help me to share that faith with others. May those around me be blessed by Your Spirit as they see You at work. Let the power, love, and self-discipline You've given show through me for Your glory.

Spending More Time with God

But I will hope continually, and will yet praise thee more and more. My mouth shall shew forth thy righteousness and thy salvation all the day; for I know not the numbers thereof. I will go in the strength of the Lord God: I will make mention of thy righteousness, even of thine only. O God, thou hast taught me from my youth: and hitherto have I declared thy wondrous works. . . . I will also praise thee with the psaltery, even thy truth, O my God: unto thee will I sing with the harp, O thou Holy One of Israel. My lips shall greatly rejoice when I sing unto thee; and my soul, which thou hast redeemed.

PSALM 71:14–17, 22–23 KJV

What motivates you to spend time praising the Lord?

....

....

....

As Christians, we sometimes say to praise the Lord for anything good that happens. This isn't a bad thing, but what is real praise? Is it just speaking the words, or is it only when we spend quality time showing God our gratitude?

....

....

....

In an age of "instant gratification," what should be our attitude toward spending more time in communication with God?

....

....

....

....

....

How do you make more time for God? What are some things you could give up so you could spend time in prayer?

....

....

....

....

As you pray, ask God to show you how to make your prayer life deeper and your time with Him more productive, and what might be standing in the way of spending time with Him.

....

....

....

....

Lord, forgive me for rushing through my prayer time. It seems there's never enough time to do all the things I need to do or want to do. Sometimes I forfeit my time with You to do something I want to do. I know that's wrong, and I want to do better. I don't thank You enough for all You do for me. Help me to be aware of all Your blessings on my life and to take the time to praise You for them. Help me not just speak words but praise You from my heart. I know there are areas of my life that could be better used in prayer time. Show me those places. Teach me how to have a deeper walk with You, and create in me a desire for more time with You.

A Grain of Mustard Seed

Another parable put he forth unto them, saying, The kingdom of heaven is like to a grain of mustard seed, which a man took, and sowed in his field: which indeed is the least of all seeds: but when it is grown, it is the greatest among herbs, and becometh a tree, so that the birds of the air come and lodge in the branches thereof. . . . And whatsoever ye do, do it heartily, as to the Lord, and not unto men.

MATTHEW 13:31–32; COLOSSIANS 3:23 KJV

What are some tasks you've completed that afterward you felt that you had wasted your time and that they had no real value? Were these feelings the result of not receiving any recognition, or did someone say something derogatory about the job you did?

....

....

....

....

In the parable of the mustard seed, Jesus taught that even the least of all seeds could develop into something worthwhile. The seed grew into a tree that provided a home for birds. What do you think Jesus was trying to tell us about the responsibilities or tasks we take on?

....

....

....

....

What does your mustard seed look like? You may think it won't amount to much, but given time and God's blessing, it may be a source of encouragement or even life to someone who's searching for a place to lodge in his or her Christian walk.

....

....

....

....

....

If you've been given a mustard seed, plant it. During prayer, ask God to bless the seed and produce something pleasing to Him, and then leave the finished product up to Him.

....

....

....

....

....

Jesus, sometimes I feel like I don't do anything worthwhile for You. I don't have the gifts or abilities that others have. Some people are so gifted and knowledgeable. The things I do seem so unimportant. What is it You would have me do? Help me to quit focusing on what I want to do and what others will think about it. Forgive me for wanting to receive recognition for the work I do. Help me to work for You that You might be glorified. Take away the desire for people to recognize me or applaud me. Without You, I am nothing. Give me the courage to plant the seed You've given me, and help me to leave the results up to You.

Through Grace

But because of his great love for us, God, who is rich in mercy, made us alive with Christ even when we were dead in transgressions—it is by grace you have been saved. And God raised us up with Christ and seated us with him in the heavenly realms in Christ Jesus, in order that in the coming ages he might show the incomparable riches of his grace, expressed in his kindness to us in Christ Jesus. For it is by grace you have been saved, through faith—and this is not from yourselves, it is the gift of God—not by works, so that no one can boast. For we are God's handiwork, created in Christ Jesus to do good works, which God prepared in advance for us to do.

EPHESIANS 2:4–10 NIV

None of us are worthy of God's great love for us. He extended mercy to us even though we didn't deserve it. That mercy changed our lives. Ask God to lead you to someone who needs His mercy.

....

....

....

....

You have been made alive with Christ. What does this life mean to you?

....

....

....

....

We're saved by grace, through faith. We can't save ourselves. It's a gift from God. How has this gift of grace changed your life?

....

....

....

What does it mean that we are created in Christ Jesus to do good works? Do you feel you are doing what God prepared in advance for you to do?

....

....

....

In prayer, ask God to lead you into the plan He prepared for you.

....

....

....

Thank You, God, for loving me. You extended mercy to me when I was unworthy of receiving such a wonderful gift. You have changed my life in so many ways. You've made me alive in Christ. Thank You for the grace that saved me and for the faith to believe that I could be saved. Lord, lead me to others who need this same grace. Help me to share Your love with them. I know that You have a plan for me, that You created me to do good works. Show me what You would have me do and give me a willing heart to follow Your plan. Sometimes I have my own ideas about what I should be doing, but help me to put aside my ideas and listen with an open heart to Your voice.

Keeping the Unity of the Spirit

As a prisoner for the Lord, then, I urge you to live a life worthy of the calling you have received. Be completely humble and gentle; be patient, bearing with one another in love. Make every effort to keep the unity of the Spirit through the bond of peace. There is one body and one Spirit, just as you were called to one hope when you were called; one Lord, one faith, one baptism; one God and Father of all, who is over all and through all and in all.

EPHESIANS 4:1–6 NIV

What is the calling all Christians have received? Paul told believers to live a life worthy of this calling. What are you doing to live a life worthy of that calling?

....

....

....

This passage tells us to be completely humble, gentle, and patient with others. Sometimes that's hard to do. If you're finding it hard to be humble, gentle, and patient, talk to God about it in prayer, asking for His help.

....

....

....

What does it mean to "keep the unity of the Spirit through the bond of peace"? How can you make the effort to do this?

....

....

....

....

....

It seems some people don't want peace. They enjoy stirring up trouble. If you know someone like this, pray for that person.

....

....

....

....

We may not want to admit it, but sometimes we are the problem instead of the solution. The more time we spend talking and listening to God, the more apt we are to become a part of the solution. If you discover you're the problem, what can you do about it?

....

....

....

....

Lord, how do I live a life worthy of the calling I've received? Your Word says we are to be humble, gentle, and patient with others. If that's how I'm to live worthy of my calling, that's a big order. Some of those people are hard to love. I have trouble being patient with them. I can't do it by myself. Help me to love them through You. Give me a gentle heart toward them, a heart that bears with others in spite of how they treat me. Help me to live a worthy life for You. Help me to pursue peace and to work at keeping unity among those around me. Show me how to be part of the solution and not part of the problem.

Don't Worry about Tomorrow

So do not worry, saying, "What shall we eat?" or "What shall we drink?" or "What shall we wear?" For the pagans run after all these things, and your heavenly Father knows that you need them. But seek first his kingdom and his righteousness, and all these things will be given to you as well. Therefore do not worry about tomorrow, for tomorrow will worry about itself. Each day has enough trouble of its own.

MATTHEW 6:31–34 NIV

What kinds of things are you worried about today?

....

....

....

....

....

It's easy to tell others not to worry about something, but when it's our time to face trouble, we find it hard to keep from worrying. In other words, it's not easy to practice what we preach. But if we believe God's Word, then we can rest assured that He knows what we're facing and how bad it is. How do we put this faith into action? How do we start practicing what we've been preaching?

....

....

....

....

....

This passage of scripture instructs us to seek God's kingdom and His righteousness first. If we do so, then the Bible tells us that we don't have to worry about tomorrow. How do you seek God's kingdom and His righteousness?

....

....

....

....

....

Don't borrow trouble from tomorrow. It may never come. Let God take charge of each day, starting today.

....

....

....

....

....

Lord, I'm worried about so many things. What are we going to do about the bills we need to pay? Where are we going to get the money to buy the things we need? I know we haven't always made good decisions in the past, but I'm asking You to help us get through this tough time. Your Word tells us not to worry about what we're going to eat or what we have to wear, but they are necessities, Lord. I don't know how to solve this problem, but I'm putting my faith and trust in You. Help me to seek You, to put You first in my life. Show me how to trust You to take care of each day. Show me how to live one day at a time with my faith in You.

Do What He Tells You

On the third day a wedding took place at Cana in Galilee.
Jesus' mother was there, and Jesus and his disciples had
also been invited to the wedding. When the wine was gone,
Jesus' mother said to him, "They have no more wine."
"Woman, why do you involve me?" Jesus replied.
"My hour has not yet come." His mother said to
the servants, "Do whatever he tells you." . . .
Jesus said to the servants, "Fill the jars with
water"; so they filled them to the brim.

JOHN 2:1–5, 7 NIV

Sometimes God may speak to your heart and ask you to do something you don't want to do. What are some of the reasons you may not want to do what He asks?

....

....

....

....

As humans, we're conscious of what others think about us. If God asks something unusual of us, pride sometimes gets in the way of being obedient to Him. If you've experienced this feeling, pray about it, asking God to help you be obedient to His voice and not so concerned with what others think.

....

....

....

....

Jesus' mother knew He had the power to solve the problem of no wine at the wedding. She told the servants to do whatever He asked them to do. How willing are you to do whatever He asks of you?

....

....

....

....

....

We don't have to be afraid of what God may ask of us. He has our best interest at heart. When the servants obeyed Jesus, the problem was solved. Ask God to give you an obedient heart to do whatever He tells you.

....

....

....

....

....

God, this thing You've asked me to do scares me. I'm afraid of what people might think or say. They may think I'm crazy. I want to obey You, but fear has me paralyzed into worrying about how I'll be received. I need Your help. I can't do this on my own. You've never asked anything of me that You didn't then help me do, but this time, I guess pride is getting in the way. Please take away the pride that keeps me from obeying You. Let the first desire of my heart be to please You and not others. Make me strong enough to step out and do whatever You tell me to do. Help me to do it for Your glory and not to receive any praise for myself or others.

A United Heart

Among the gods there is none like unto thee, O Lord;
neither are there any works like unto thy works. All nations
whom thou hast made shall come and worship before thee,
O Lord; and shall glorify thy name. For thou art great, and doest
wondrous things: thou art God alone. Teach me thy way, O LORD;
I will walk in thy truth: unite my heart to fear thy name. I will
praise thee, O Lord my God, with all my heart: and I will glorify
thy name for evermore. For great is thy mercy toward me:
and thou hast delivered my soul from the lowest hell.

PSALM 86:8–13 KJV

What are the works of the Lord that give you the knowledge and confidence that there is no other god like Him?

....

....

....

In your prayer time today, take time to praise God and acknowledge His works in your life and the lives of those around you.

....

....

....

The psalmist said he would walk in God's truth. How are you walking in God's truth? If you need more knowledge of His truth, ask Him to show you His ways.

....

....

....

....

....

Is your heart united to fear God's name? Sometimes our hearts are divided on what we should do. A part of us wants to follow the natural, fleshly desires. The other part wants to follow God. If your heart isn't united to fear God's name, spend time in prayer asking God to unite your heart to follow Him.

....

....

....

....

God desires to hear us praise Him. Spend some time praising Him for His mercy toward you.

....

....

....

....

God, I know there is no one else like You. Your work is all around me. I see it in my life and the lives of other people. Your creation is full of color and living, breathing things. I glorify Thy name today for the great and wonderful works that You do. No one else can do what You do. Teach me how to follow You. I want to know Your ways. Unite my heart to serve and worship You. Take away all the things that divide my heart, and give me a heart of praise for You. Thank You for showing me mercy and providing the gift of salvation so that I might be saved. You're worthy of all my praise.

Are Your Bones Dry?

*And he said unto me, Son of man, can these bones live?
And I answered, O Lord God, thou knowest. . . . Thus saith the
Lord God unto these bones; Behold, I will cause breath to enter
into you, and ye shall live: and I will lay sinews upon you, and will
bring up flesh upon you, and cover you with skin, and put breath
in you, and ye shall live; and ye shall know that I am the Lord. . . .
So I prophesied as he commanded me, and the breath
came into them, and they lived, and stood up
upon their feet, an exceeding great army.*
Ezekiel 37:3, 5–6, 10 KJV

If you feel you're spinning your wheels without going anywhere in your Christian walk, your spiritual bones may be dry. As women, we wear several hats that require much from us. We can become dry without realizing it.

No one else may know or realize what you're experiencing, but God does. You can talk to Him about your condition. Ask Him to breathe life back into your walk with Him.

The act of restoration may be greater than you realize, but trust God to supply all that you need to become a healthy, vibrant Christian again.

....

....

....

....

....

When the prophet Ezekiel obeyed the Lord and prophesied to the dry bones, new breath came into them, and they became alive once more and stood up as a great army. As you obey God's voice and allow Him to breathe fresh life into you, you'll become a part of His great army again. How can you allow God to breathe fresh life into you?

....

....

....

....

....

Lord, I'm not getting anywhere in my walk with You. I feel like I'm spinning my wheels. I feel dry and empty. It seems that everyone requires something from me and I can't find time to talk to You. Sometimes I'd like to run away and hide from all the demands on my life. I feel like Ezekiel's dry bones, used up and lifeless. Please breathe life into my dead bones and restore me to good spiritual health. Give me wisdom to know which demands I should give in to and which I should say no to so that I won't become drained and dry again. Breathe fresh life into me so I can be the person You want me to be.

You Are God's Temple

Don't you know that you yourselves are God's temple and that God's Spirit dwells in your midst? If anyone destroys God's temple, God will destroy that person; for God's temple is sacred, and you together are that temple. Do not deceive yourselves. If any of you think you are wise by the standards of this age, you should become "fools" so that you may become wise. For the wisdom of this world is foolishness in God's sight. As it is written: "He catches the wise in their craftiness"; and again, "The Lord knows that the thoughts of the wise are futile."

1 Corinthians 3:16–20 niv

If we are God's temple, then our lifestyle should reflect Him and the way He wants us to conduct ourselves. Many forces try to lure us away from being godly women. What can you do to resist these ideas?

....

....

....

The world has a standard by which it measures women, from the way we perform at work to how we treat other people to how we dress. What standards should we set for ourselves in light of what the Bible teaches us?

....

....

....

....

We are surrounded by the call of the world. What voices are you hearing, and what can you do to silence them? Take time to hear God's voice when He speaks to you.

....

....

....

The wisdom of the world is foolishness to God. Ask God for His wisdom so you will know how to be wise for Him.

....

....

....

If you are to be God's temple, ask Him to make you a place He would be pleased to dwell in.

....

....

....

Lord, there are so many temptations all around me. I want to be the kind of woman You want me to be, but sometimes I feel pulled in the wrong direction. Other women don't seem to be bothered by the way they dress or act, but I want to be pleasing to You. Help me to take my eyes off what others are doing so I can do what I know pleases You. Help me to be strong enough to set higher standards for myself. Give me wisdom to know how to live in this world and how to conduct myself as a godly woman. Make me a godly temple where You will be pleased to live.

Jars of Clay

Therefore, since through God's mercy we have this ministry, we do not lose heart. Rather, we have renounced secret and shameful ways; we do not use deception, nor do we distort the word of God. . . . For what we preach is not ourselves, but Jesus Christ as Lord, and ourselves as your servants for Jesus' sake. For God, who said, "Let light shine out of darkness," made his light shine in our hearts to give us the light of the knowledge of God's glory displayed in the face of Christ. But we have this treasure in jars of clay to show that this all-surpassing power is from God and not from us.

2 Corinthians 4:1–2, 5–7 NIV

What are some ways you are sharing Christ with others?

....

....

....

....

How receptive are others to your message about Christ and what He has done in your life? Why do you think they are or are not receptive?

....

....

....

....

As witnesses for Christ, we must be sure that we do not distort the Word of God. To ensure that you share only the truth, ask God to open your understanding of His Word.

....

....

....

Whatever we share with others must be evident in our own lives. The light of Christ must shine through us to those we speak to. In your prayer time, ask God to let His light shine through you for others to receive Him.

....

....

....

If we are led by God's Spirit, then He can do a work in other people's lives as we share the Gospel with them. His Word and work in our lives is a special treasure that comes from God. We cannot take credit for what God does. How can we give Him the credit that belongs to Him?

....

....

....

Lord, I want to lead other people to You. Help me as I share with others what You have done in my life. Help me not to share anything that is not from You. As I read Your Word, open my understanding, not just for myself, but so I can share it with others. You know who needs to hear my testimony; direct me to them. Place them in my path and help me to be sensitive to Your Spirit so I will know what I need to say. I have no power to transform anyone. Only You can do that. Thank You for placing this treasure inside of me, a simple jar of clay.

Pray Anyway

Save me, O God, for the waters have come up to my neck. I sink in the miry depths, where there is no foothold. I have come into the deep waters; the floods engulf me. I am worn out calling for help; my throat is parched. My eyes fail, looking for my God. Those who hate me without reason outnumber the hairs of my head; many are my enemies without cause, those who seek to destroy me. I am forced to restore what I did not steal. You, God, know my folly; my guilt is not hidden from you.

PSALM 69:1–5 NIV

Sometimes it can feel as if we're drowning in trouble and there's no one to rescue us. What thoughts cross your mind during a time like that? Commit those thoughts to God and ask Him for faith to believe that He will save you from the waters that are up to your neck.

....

....

....

If you feel like God isn't listening to you, spend time in prayer thanking Him and praising Him despite your feelings. He tells us in His Word that we will find Him when we search with all our heart (Jeremiah 29:13).

....

....

....

Often when we are depressed or going through a bad time, we feel like God is going to be too late with His answer. These are the times we need to trust that He hears us even when we can't sense His presence. How can we learn to wait on Him and not be impatient?

....

....

....

When you feel "used" by others and think that life isn't fair, what can you do to change your mind-set and think more positive thoughts?

....

....

....

When you pray, believe that God hears you no matter what the situation looks like.

....

....

....

Jesus, help me. I don't know what to do about the situations in my life. I feel like I'm drowning and no one cares. I keep praying about this problem, but You're not answering me. You know I need help. The people around me don't understand what I'm going through. Some of them have turned against me. It hurts so much to be treated this way. Even though I can't feel You, I'm trying to believe that You're going to work out my problems. I can't do this alone, Lord, so I'm asking for strength to make it through this time and for faith to believe that You will be with me whatever happens.

Small Things

Jesus replied, "They do not need to go away. You give them something to eat." "We have here only five loaves of bread and two fish," they answered. "Bring them here to me," he said. And he directed the people to sit down on the grass. Taking the five loaves and the two fish and looking up to heaven, he gave thanks and broke the loaves. Then he gave them to the disciples, and the disciples gave them to the people. They all ate and were satisfied, and the disciples picked up twelve basketfuls of broken pieces that were left over. The number of those who ate was about five thousand men, besides women and children.

MATTHEW 14:16–21 NIV

What are you concerned about today? Make a list of what is bothering you, no matter what it is; then pray over the list.

....

....

....

....

Sometimes the things we worry about may seem small to others—maybe they even seem small to us—but not to Jesus. Talk to Him about your problem. He won't consider it too small. He's interested in what concerns us.

....

....

....

....

Jesus had compassion on the people who had come to listen to Him. He knew they needed food, and He didn't let them go hungry. He took care of the problem. If you believe that He will take care of your problem, spend some time giving Him thanks in advance for His provision.

....

....

....

....

....

The feeding of the five-thousand-plus crowd was a miracle. If you believe in miracles, ask God for faith to believe that He can do the same for you.

....

....

....

....

....

Jesus, You know what I need today. You know what I'm concerned about. It may seem like a small thing to other people, but I'm worried about it. If You supplied something as basic as a meal for the crowd gathered to hear You, then I know You're concerned about my situation too. Give me faith to believe for my small problems as well as the big things. I know You can work miracles in my life just as You did for those in Your day. Thank You for being concerned for me. Thank You for always supplying what I need.

Enriched by God

For in him you have been enriched in every way—with all kinds of speech and with all knowledge—God thus confirming our testimony about Christ among you. Therefore you do not lack any spiritual gift as you eagerly wait for our Lord Jesus Christ to be revealed. He will also keep you firm to the end, so that you will be blameless on the day of our Lord Jesus Christ. God is faithful, who has called you into fellowship with his Son, Jesus Christ our Lord. I appeal to you, brothers and sisters, in the name of our Lord Jesus Christ, that all of you agree with one another in what you say and that there be no divisions among you, but that you be perfectly united in mind and thought.

1 CORINTHIANS 1:5–10 NIV

God has blessed and enriched His people with spiritual gifts—all kinds of speech and knowledge. What are some of the gifts you feel God has blessed you with? How are you using the gifts and abilities He has given you?

....

....

....

If you don't recognize any particular ability or gift, ask God to show you the gifts He wants to give you. Sometimes we have our own idea about what kind of ability or gift we want God to give us. Pray about those feelings and allow God to do the choosing for you.

....

....

....

What should be your attitude toward these gifts, knowing they came from God and not any natural ability of your own?

....

....

....

....

If you are involved in a church or fellowship where there is some division, ask God for wisdom to know what to do and say.

....

....

....

....

How do we become perfectly united in mind and thought?

....

....

....

....

Lord, thank You for the spiritual gifts You have given me and others around me. Help me to recognize that they are from You and that I have nothing to brag about in myself. Help me to use the abilities and gifts You've given me so they will glorify You and not me. Help me to have the right attitude about what You want me to do. Take away any pride or division that might hinder Your work in my life or Your church. Unite us by Your Spirit so the gifts and abilities You have given will benefit Your kingdom.

Let God Do the Promoting

To the arrogant I say, "Boast no more," and to the wicked,
"Do not lift up your horns. Do not lift your horns against heaven;
do not speak so defiantly." No one from the east or the west
or from the desert can exalt themselves. It is God who judges:
He brings one down, he exalts another. . . . For by the grace given
me I say to every one of you: Do not think of yourself more highly
than you ought, but rather think of yourself with sober judgment,
in accordance with the faith God has distributed to each of you.

Psalm 75:4–7; Romans 12:3 niv

As a Christian, what should be your attitude about boastful speaking or "tooting your own horn"? Is there ever a time when Christians should promote themselves to get ahead?

....

....

....

What are some times it might be okay to speak about an accomplishment in your life?

....

....

....

If you've ever been passed over for a promotion or position, how did you feel? What kind of thoughts passed through your mind? Did you allow those thoughts to take root? If you're still troubled by those thoughts and feelings, take them to God in prayer.

....

....

....

....

....

The scripture passage today says we can't exalt ourselves. God is
the judge; He decides who should be promoted and who shouldn't.
How do you feel about that?

....

....

....

....

If you were passed over for something you thought you deserved,
what was your attitude? If you know you had the wrong attitude,
ask God for help.

....

....

....

....

*Jesus, I'm disappointed because I didn't receive the position I wanted.
I know that You know best, but I can't help but feel hurt. I know You
have my best interest at heart and I need to accept that this is Your
will for my life. I'm having trouble accepting that the other person
is more deserving than I am. I've had all kinds of thoughts about the
outcome of this situation, and I need to repent of those thoughts.
Forgive me for thinking bad about the other person. Help that person
to do a good job, and help me to accept this as Your will. I know
You have good things for me in the future. Give me the courage to
accept Your will for my life and not get in the way of Your work.*

Speak Truth

*These are the things that ye shall do; Speak ye every man
the truth to his neighbour; execute the judgment of truth
and peace in your gates: and let none of you imagine evil
in your hearts against his neighbour; and love no false
oath: for all these are things that I hate, saith the LORD.*

ZECHARIAH 8:16–17 KJV

Twenty-first-century culture seems to think it's okay to color the truth to protect yourself or someone else. How important is it to you to speak truth? How does it make you feel when someone lies to you?

....

....

....

It's all too easy sometimes to slip into the habits of those around you, believing that "it's just the way things are." What can you do to keep this from happening in your life? Ask God for direction by His Spirit to resist slipping into these habits.

....

....

....

Jesus taught that our neighbor isn't just those who live next door to us. It's everyone we come in contact with. In light of this thought, how should we treat both those who live around us and anyone we meet?

....

....

....

....

The imagination is a wonderful thing unless it's used for evil purposes. This passage of scripture instructs us not to imagine evil in our hearts against our neighbor. If we are to execute peace and truth, our thoughts must remain pure. How can we keep our imagination from going down the wrong path?

....

....

....

God says He hates lying and evil imaginations. The world believes in gray areas. How should Christians feel about this?

....

....

....

Lord, Your Word tells us to speak truth to those around us. So many people see nothing wrong with telling what they call a little white lie. I know You don't approve of lying in any form. Help me to always tell the truth—even when it hurts, no matter what others think or do. Keep me sensitive to Your Spirit so I will know how to conduct my life. Don't let me become so used to what the world is like that it creeps up on me. Keep me from those habits that are displeasing to You. Help me to show respect for my neighbor and all those around me. Give me a pure mind and a pure heart so I won't imagine evil against anyone. Give me the courage to execute peace and truth in every situation.

Pray for Your Enemies

"You have heard that it was said, 'Love your neighbor and hate your enemy.' But I tell you, love your enemies and pray for those who persecute you, that you may be children of your Father in heaven. He causes his sun to rise on the evil and the good, and sends rain on the righteous and the unrighteous. If you love those who love you, what reward will you get? Are not even the tax collectors doing that? And if you greet only your own people, what are you doing more than others? Do not even pagans do that?"

MATTHEW 5:43–47 NIV

It's easy to turn a small molehill of misunderstanding into a mountain of bitterness and resentment. When we allow the incident to grow, we lose perspective and begin to consider the other person an enemy. Take time to pray about the situation, asking God to help you see things more clearly.

....

....

....

When someone hurts us, it's easy to feel sorry for ourselves and to feel justified in doing so. Jesus told us that we should pray for those who have caused us pain. Who has hurt or persecuted you in some way? Even though it may be one of the hardest things you've ever done, start praying for them.

....

....

....

Jesus said if we love only those who love us, what kind of reward will we get? When we spend time only with those we love, we feel safe. We are content to stay in our comfort zone. We're not doing anything the rest of the world doesn't do. Likewise, if we only speak to our own family and friends, what are we doing more than others? Even unbelievers do that. Write out a prayer asking God to help you reach out to those outside your group.

....

....

....

....

....

....

....

....

....

Jesus, You know the people in my life who have hurt me or made me angry. I've tried to justify the way I feel toward them, but I know You're not pleased with the way I'm handling this matter. Open my eyes and show me how to turn this wrong into a right. Forgive me for the resentment I've felt, and help me love them as You would have me love them. Bless them, Lord, and make Yourself known to them so they can experience peace through You. Help me to reach out to those outside my family and my group of friends.

Pray for Healing

Is any sick among you? let him call for the elders of the church; and let them pray over him, anointing him with oil in the name of the Lord: and the prayer of faith shall save the sick, and the Lord shall raise him up; and if he have committed sins, they shall be forgiven him.

JAMES 5:14–15 KJV

These verses in James teach us that if we're sick, we should ask the leaders of our church to anoint us with oil and pray for us. How do you feel about asking someone to pray for you? How do you feel about divine healing?

....

....

....

If you've never asked for prayer for a physical healing, what is your reason? Are you worried about what other people will think, or is it hard for you to believe that healing is possible? Whatever your reason, pray about it in your private prayer time, telling God exactly how you feel.

....

....

....

How is the prayer of faith different from any other prayer? If you feel you need more faith, ask God to supply the faith you need.

....

....

....

....

God uses people to carry out His work on earth, but we have no power outside of God's Spirit working in us. Only God has the power to work miracles of healing. Our faith must be in Him, not those who are praying.

....

....

....

Sometimes people aren't healed. How should this affect our feelings about intercession if someone doesn't receive what he or she needs after prayer; should we stop asking? In your prayer time, ask God for guidance to believe in His ability to heal, and then leave the results up to Him.

....

....

....

Lord, I need healing for the problem I'm having, but I don't understand everything about healing. You know and understand my condition. I've never asked anyone to pray for me before, so I'm not sure about that. Help me not to be afraid. Your Word teaches that we should ask for prayer. I know that You care about me and that You want the best for me. Help me to know what to do about my situation. Give me the faith to believe that You can heal my body. I've seen other people healed, so I know You can do it. Help me to rely on You, to have faith in You whether I receive healing or not. The reasons belong to You.

Ask for Wisdom

If any of you lacks wisdom, you should ask God, who gives generously to all without finding fault, and it will be given to you. But when you ask, you must believe and not doubt, because the one who doubts is like a wave of the sea, blown and tossed by the wind. That person should not expect to receive anything from the Lord. Such a person is double-minded and unstable in all they do.

JAMES 1:5–8 NIV

What are some reasons you might feel you need more wisdom?

....

....

....

We need wisdom in every area of our lives. There is a worldly wisdom that the world knows, but we also need godly wisdom to live for God. What kind of wisdom was James speaking about in this passage?

....

....

....

Don't be ashamed or embarrassed to ask God for wisdom. He won't hold it against you. He is a generous God, and He wants to give you what you need to live your daily life and to walk with Him. Ask God for the wisdom you need.

....

....

....

When you ask God for something, believe in Him. He honors faith. James wrote that the person who doubts is like a wave of the sea, blown around by the wind. Think about what wind does to water. How does this pertain to your life?

....

....

....

....

....

If you are having trouble with doubt, ask God to remove the doubt and strengthen your faith in Him, giving you stability in your Christian walk.

....

....

....

....

....

Lord, I've made a lot of mistakes. I need wisdom so I can make good decisions in my job, my family, and my walk with You. Please give me the wisdom I need in my life. Help me to believe that You can meet this need; take away any doubt that might be holding back the wisdom I know You want to give me. Give me stability in my walk with You. Help me to be a woman who walks in wisdom, not one who stumbles from one decision to another or allows the winds of the world to shake her foundation. Direct my steps and make me wise for Your glory.

A Sober Mind

Be alert and of sober mind. Your enemy the devil prowls around like a roaring lion looking for someone to devour. Resist him, standing firm in the faith, because you know that the family of believers throughout the world is undergoing the same kind of sufferings. And the God of all grace, who called you to his eternal glory in Christ, after you have suffered a little while, will himself restore you and make you strong, firm and steadfast.

1 Peter 5:8–10 NIV

Verse 8 tells us to be of sober mind. What does it mean to have a sober mind?

....

....

....

The devil is our enemy, and he wants to destroy us. He prowls around looking for a victim. We must be alert at all times and keep a sober mind. Spend time in prayer, asking God to keep you alert and help you have a sober mind.

....

....

....

The way to resist the devil is to stand firm in the faith. If you are having trouble standing firm, ask God to help you become stronger in your faith.

....

....

Sometimes when the enemy comes against us, we tend to feel like we're the only one he's bothering. But Peter said that believers throughout the world are going through the same kind of suffering. Allowing self-pity to creep in can weaken your resistance to the devil. Ask God to take away any feelings of self-pity you may be experiencing. Don't allow those feelings to creep back in.

There is hope in the middle of all the trials. God will restore you and make you strong and steadfast, helping you to resist the enemy. Spend time in prayer, asking God to strengthen you.

Lord, give me a sober mind, one that is focused on You. Keep me aware of what is going on around me. Help me to be alert to the devil's tricks and his deceptions. Give me the strength and faith I need to resist him, and help me to stand firm in that faith. Forgive me for allowing self-pity to creep in. I know there are other people who are going through temptations and problems just like I am. Give us the strength we need to stand against the devil. Thank You for Your grace. I know You will restore me and make me a strong Christian. Help me to stand for You in every situation.

He Is the Potter

All of us have become like one who is unclean, and all our righteous acts are like filthy rags; we all shrivel up like a leaf, and like the wind our sins sweep us away. No one calls on your name or strives to lay hold of you; for you have hidden your face from us and have given us over to our sins. Yet you, Lord, are our Father. We are the clay, you are the potter; we are all the work of your hand.

Isaiah 64:6–8 NIV

Why did the writer of this passage call our righteous acts filthy rags?

....

....

....

....

....

When we spend time talking to God, He can show us where we have failed to live as He would have us to. If you find yourself in this position today, you may need to set aside time to spend in prayer. Our pride doesn't always want to acknowledge that we have done wrong, but if we ask God for help, He will reveal our need to repent and be reconciled to Him.

....

....

....

....

....

A potter places a lump of clay on a potter's wheel and begins to mold it with his hands. God is our Potter, and we are that lump of clay sitting on the wheel. What are you willing for God to do in your life to mold you into a vessel that pleases Him?

....

....

....

....

Sometimes the clay isn't pliable in the potter's hands. He has to start over to mold the clay. We might be tempted to take ourselves off the potter's wheel because the shaping and molding becomes painful. But if we allow Him to mold us, God will make us into a useful vessel for His kingdom. How can you be pliable in His hands?

....

....

....

....

God, I know that all of my good works can never make me righteous or earn me a place in heaven. There is nothing in me that is clean without You. I know I have failed You by allowing sin into my life. Please forgive me and take away the desires that are not pleasing to You. You are my Potter. Without You, I'm a lifeless lump of clay. Take my life into Your capable hands and mold me into a vessel that can be used for Your glory. Help me to be willing to stay on the potter's wheel, no matter how painful it may be, until I am shaped into Your image.

Bearing Fruit

*So I say, walk by the Spirit, and you will not gratify the
desires of the flesh. . . . But the fruit of the Spirit is love,
joy, peace, forbearance, kindness, goodness, faithfulness,
gentleness and self-control. Against such things there
is no law. Those who belong to Christ Jesus have crucified
the flesh with its passions and desires. Since we live
by the Spirit, let us keep in step with the Spirit.*

GALATIANS 5:16, 22–25 NIV

If the Holy Spirit dwells in us, we should bear fruit that comes through His work in our lives. How are you allowing Him to work in your life so that you bear fruit?

....

....

....

As you read through the list of the fruit of the Spirit, you may feel some are missing from your life. What makes you feel this way?

....

....

....

Producing all this fruit is a tall order for us on our own. In fact, we cannot do this ourselves. The Holy Spirit produces the fruit as we allow Him to control our lives. As you spend time in prayer, ask Him to take control in those areas where you are lacking.

....

....

....

....

If we belong to Jesus, we must crucify or kill fleshly desires that keep us from being clean and holy before Christ. If you have desires that you know are wrong, commit them to Christ in prayer, seeking His help for deliverance.

....

....

....

If we are going to live in the Spirit, we must walk in the Spirit. This means we do the bidding of the Holy Spirit in our lives on a daily basis. As we walk with Him, we become like Him.

....

....

....

Father, I want to be a fruit bearer. I want the Holy Spirit to take control of my life so that I can bear fruit pleasing to You. You know what I'm in need of. You know which of the fruit is missing and what I need to do to have that fruit become a part of my walk with You. Forgive me for going my own way and allowing desires and passions to continue in my life that I know shouldn't be there. Help me to live and walk in Your Spirit every day. Let the fruit of the Spirit become a part of my life.

What Are You Pressing Toward?

*Brethren, I count not myself to have apprehended: but this
one thing I do, forgetting those things which are behind,
and reaching forth unto those things which are before,
I press toward the mark for the prize of the high calling of
God in Christ Jesus. . . . For our conversation is in heaven;
from whence also we look for the Saviour, the Lord Jesus Christ.*
PHILIPPIANS 3:13–14, 20 KJV

Paul had worked hard for God, but he didn't feel he had it made. He had not reached his goal. There may have been those around him who thought he was a success, but he didn't allow himself to fall into that trap. He knew he still had work to do. How can we keep the right attitude about our accomplishments?

....

....

....

Paul wasn't always a believer. He had done some bad things in his life, but he said he was forgetting about those things. He could only do that because of Christ in his life. If there are things in your past that bother you, pray about them, asking Jesus to help you put those things behind you.

....

....

....

When a runner is in a race and headed for the finish line, he makes an extra effort to reach that goal. He presses toward that mark. What are you doing to press toward your goal in Christ? Maybe, like the runner, you need to make an extra effort to reach the mark.

....

....

....

....

Sometimes we're prone to allow what others think of us or our past to slow us in our progress. Don't let the enemy distract you. Keep your eyes on the finish line.

....

....

....

....

As you pray, ask God for strength to remain in the race for the heavenly finish line.

....

....

....

....

Lord, You know all about my past. There's nothing I've done that You don't know about. You've already forgiven me for those things, but they still bother me sometimes. Help me to put the past behind me and forget about it. Help me not to listen to the enemy when he tries to bring it up again. Give me strength to press toward the mark You have set for me. Help me to stay in the race and not give up. Guide my steps so I won't stumble and fall, but keep running to the end.

The Truth Sets You Free

To the Jews who had believed him, Jesus said, "If you hold to
my teaching, you are really my disciples. Then you will know
the truth, and the truth will set you free." They answered him,
"We are Abraham's descendants and have never been slaves
of anyone. How can you say that we shall be set free?"
Jesus replied, "Very truly I tell you, everyone who sins
is a slave to sin. . . . So if the Son sets you
free, you will be free indeed."
JOHN 8:31–34, 36 NIV

There are many different teachings in the world today. Jesus told those who believed in Him that if they held to His teachings, they were His disciples. How can you be sure that the teachings you hear are Jesus' teachings? When you pray, ask Jesus to show you His truth.

....

....

....

Jesus said, "The truth will set you free." What kind of truth was He speaking about? How does knowing this truth make a difference in your life?

....

....

....

The Jews thought Jesus was speaking about natural, physical bondage or slavery. Because they were Abraham's descendants, they thought they were free. Nothing we do or become can make us free in Christ. Jesus wanted the Jews to experience His freedom, and He wants you to experience it also. How can we know we are free?

....

....

....

How does being set free by the Son make you free indeed? How does it make your life different from unbelievers?

....

....

....

Does being set free mean we can live any way we want to?

....

....

....

Jesus, thank You for setting me free with Your truth. Without You, I would still be a slave to sin and my old life. Keep me in Your truth. Don't allow me to be deceived by false teachings or by those who claim to know the truth but are really in bondage. Open my understanding as I read Your Word and learn more about You. Let Your truth take root in my life and guide me on a daily basis. Thank You for the freedom that I have in You; show me how to live in this freedom that You've provided so I won't stray into my own will. Help me to share Your truth with others who need to be set free.

Showing Gratitude

Bless the LORD, O my soul: and all that is within me, bless his holy name. Bless the LORD, O my soul, and forget not all his benefits: who forgiveth all thine iniquities; who healeth all thy diseases; who redeemeth thy life from destruction; who crowneth thee with lovingkindness and tender mercies; who satisfieth thy mouth with good things; so that thy youth is renewed like the eagle's. . . . O give thanks unto the LORD; call upon his name: make known his deeds among the people.

PSALM 103:1–5; 105:1 KJV

How thankful are you? Sometimes we go through the day without stopping to think about all that we have and where it comes from. Often our prayers consist of requests or needs, which is a necessary part of our lives, but gratitude should be a part of our prayers also.

....

....

....

What are some of the benefits that God provides for you?

....

....

....

God provides for us on a spiritual level because He has forgiven our sins through the sacrifice made by His Son on the cross. Have you thanked Him today for the gift of salvation?

....

....

....

....

The psalmist said he wanted to bless God with his whole being, all that was within him. How can you bless God with your whole being? Spend some time in prayer just thanking and blessing God for all He has done for you.

....

....

....

God not only cares for us on a spiritual level but also provides for our physical and emotional well-being. He satisfies us with good things so that we are renewed. Telling others about God's goodness is one way we can bless Him. Why not share with someone else what God has done for you?

....

....

....

Lord, forgive me for not showing You more often how much I appreciate all You've done for me. Today, I just want to spend some time blessing You and thanking You for Your goodness to me. Thank You for sending Jesus to die for me so I could have eternal life. Thank You for keeping me safe and watching over me. You've blessed me with so much mercy and many good things. Thank You for giving me new strength for each day. Help me to share Your goodness with someone else today.

Topical index

Journal Your Way to a Deeper Faith

Bible Study Map for Women

This unique journal is an engaging and creative way for you to dig deep into God's Word. Every colorful page will guide you to create your very own Bible study map as you write out specific thoughts, ideas, questions, and more, which you can follow—from start to finish!—as you study God's Word.

Spiral Bound / 978-1-64352-178-7 / $7.99

The Prayer Map for Women

This engaging prayer journal is a fun and creative way for you to more fully experience the power of prayer in your life. Each page features a lovely 2-color design that guides you to write out specific thoughts, ideas, and lists. . .which then creates a specific "map" for you to follow as you talk to God.

Spiral Bound / 978-1-68322-557-7 / $7.99